Multiverse Deism

Multiverse Deism

Shifting Perspectives of God and the World

Leland Royce Harper

LEXINGTON BOOKS
Lanham • Boulder • New York • London

Published by Lexington Books
An imprint of The Rowman & Littlefield Publishing Group, Inc.
4501 Forbes Boulevard, Suite 200, Lanham, Maryland 20706
www.rowman.com

6 Tinworth Street, London SE11 5AL, United Kingdom

Copyright © 2020 The Rowman & Littlefield Publishing Group, Inc.

All rights reserved. No part of this book may be reproduced in any form or by any electronic or mechanical means, including information storage and retrieval systems, without written permission from the publisher, except by a reviewer who may quote passages in a review.

British Library Cataloguing in Publication Information Available

Library of Congress Cataloging-in-Publication Data Is Available

Library of Congress Control Number: 2020935396

ISBN 978-1-7936-1475-9 (cloth: alk. paper)
ISBN 978-1-7936-1476-6 (electronic)

∞™ The paper used in this publication meets the minimum requirements of American National Standard for Information Sciences—Permanence of Paper for Printed Library Materials, ANSI/NISO Z39.48-1992.

Contents

Acknowledgments		vii
1	Introduction	1
2	The Case for the Multiverse	7
3	The Theist and the Multiverse	25
4	Attributes of a Deistic God	47
5	Why Being a Deist May Not Be So Bad	69
6	Possible Alternative Version of Deism	89
7	Potential Difficulties and Further Lines of Inquiry for the Multiverse Deist	107
8	Practical Considerations and Concluding Thoughts	125
References		133
Index		139
About the Author		141

Acknowledgments

The ideas presented in this project are refined versions of rough thoughts that I had put on the backburner for several years. So, when I had the opportunity to branch out from my previous research interests and begin work in the world of the multiverse and deism I was, admittedly, both excited and scared at the task ahead of me. Being able to step outside of my philosophical comfort zone and to undertake this kind of research is definitely not something that I would have been able to do without the great support system and opportunities that surrounded me.

I credit Dale Martelli for first introducing a fifteen-year-old me to philosophy at Vancouver Technical Secondary School, and in lighting that initial spark of inquiry that I will forever carry with me. Many thanks to my previous philosophy professors who all, collectively, helped to broaden my philosophical interests as a young student. I would also like to specifically thank Dr. Yujin Nagasawa and Dr. Klaas Kraay, as there is no doubt that I would not have been able to complete this project were it not for the mentorship that you were both able to provide. I could always count on you to provide me with the guidance that I needed and to point me in the right direction.

Many of the ideas contained in this project were presented or discussed at various conferences or workshops around the world. I would like to thank those conference and workshop organizers for allowing me to participate, as well as those who commented on and criticized my work, allowing me to make the necessary adjustments to my initial arguments. I would also like to thank the editorial board at *Forum Philosophicum*, as well as the reviewers, for their comments on and publication of essays that would go on to become chapter 6 in this project. The ideas expressed in this chapter are derived from two papers, entitled "A Deistic Discussion of Murphy and Tracy's Accounts of God's Limited Activity in the World" and "Epistemic Deism Revisited," that I previously authored and that were first published in *Forum Philosophicum* volumes 18 and 20; Harper (2013) and Harper (2015). They are used with permission from *Forum Philosophicum*.

Finally, I would like to thank my friends and family for providing me with all of the support, whatever kind I needed, in the pursuit of completing this research project. Most importantly, my wife Marina, my daughter Emmeline, and my son Beau. Thank you all for your love, your encouragement, and for providing me with the space and time necessary to complete this project. I know it has not been easy but you have been there at all hours of the day or night to help me with whatever I needed, and my ability complete this was largely due to your continued strength and support. This is for you.

Chapter 1

Introduction

THE PROJECT AND ITS ORIGINS

In this project, I argue for the plausibility of a deistic God, rather than the God of classical theism, given the existence of a particular kind of multiverse. Furthermore, I argue that the alternative of a deistic God has some aspects that make it preferential to the God of classical theism, specifically in standing up to certain arguments for atheism. The ideas discussed in this research project did not grow out of some long-held burning question that was within me; instead, they evolved out of several different lines of thought and interests that I explored over the past several years. The initial ideas for this research project were to examine and ultimately argue for the plausibility of deism as an alternative to classical theism and to demonstrate how a deistic conception of God could fare better against particular arguments for atheism than the traditional conception of God could. As will be seen, those ideas and discussions are maintained in this project, but they serve as a starting point for a more expanded discussion. In researching the feasibility of deism over classical theism, I still felt that there was an aspect missing, that is, there still needed to be a reason to accept deism in favor of classical theism other than merely because it may provide a better response to specific arguments for atheism. There needed to be some prior reason that called for a deistic God rather than the God of classical theism, allowing for an ontological view that would not be adopted merely as a means to reply to specific objections, but for an ontological view that would be adopted on independent grounds and would subsequently be able to satisfactorily address many objections in ways better than classical theism.

The route of providing independent justification for deism came via the multiverse, and the impact of the multiverse aspect of this project is twofold.

Firstly, the discussion of the multiverse serves as an independent method of conferring plausibility and entailment on the idea of deism. This adds a certain level of credibility to the adoption of deism as a whole and provides us with more reasons to accept deism than simply because deism may reply to certain arguments for atheism in a more effective way than does classical theism. Secondly, through the addition of the multiverse aspect, the overall theory that I propose covers far more ground than it otherwise would have were it restricted solely to a discussion of deism. Interest in alternative conceptions of God is growing within the philosophy of religion,[1] albeit with some pushback, but deism is still one of the alternative conceptions that go largely undiscussed, so the appeal of a project that only discusses deism, while useful, would be toward a very narrow section of the broader group of philosophers or religion. The multiverse is one of the most highly discussed topics within the philosophy of religion at the moment, and by adding that dimension, this project is able to appeal to a far broader group of philosophers. So, in the search for independent justification for an under-discussed alternative conception of God I turned to the highly discussed multiverse, and through this, I was able to construct a research project that explores an under-discussed area of philosophy in a way that still appeals to a broader spectrum of philosophers of religion.

STRUCTURE

I begin by presenting a survey of the current multiverse discussion, in chapter 2, from both the philosophical and the scientific perspectives. Through this, I show that the multiverse is a serious ontological view being researched by a good number of reputable individuals across different disciplines and that it ought to be given strong consideration. I also highlight the variety of different types of multiverse that are currently being discussed by philosophers and physicists, emphasizing the range of varying multiverse options that are available, while also noting that there does seem to be a general consensus on the existence of the multiverse, but that the debate arises in terms of determining the makeup of that multiverse. Furthermore, I go on to specify the kind of multiverse model that I will go on to operate with for the remainder of this research project as a model that calls for the existence of all possible universes—one roughly similar to modal realism.

Moving into the third chapter, I outline several of the difficulties that the theist faces and needs to deal with in accepting a multiverse theory that calls for the existence of all possible universes. Some of these difficulties will not be exclusive to theists, rather they will apply to anyone accepting that particular brand of multiverse theory, but they are problems that the theistic proponent of the multiverse will have to face, nonetheless. The first section of the chapter addresses the overall thesis of this research project, and details how the theistic acceptance of a multiverse theory that calls for the existence of all possible universes entails a deistic God rather than the God of classical Judeo-Christian monotheism. And finally, the chapter concludes with a presentation of how various accounts of free will and determinism play out in the multiverse when there is a deistic God, showing how multiple conceptions and combinations of free will and determinism are compatible with the deistic multiverse theory that I ultimately argue for.

Chapter 4 begins with a discussion on the vague nature of the deistic God, and some of the potential reasons behind that lack of clarity throughout history. Because of the lack of specific divine attributes or interpretations of these divine attributes within the historical literature of deism, I take the overall conception of the deistic God to be open, save for the fact that He does not intervene in the natural world. Moving into sections aptly entitled *Omnipotence* and *Omnibenevolence* I discuss my interpretations of omnipotence and omnibenevolence, which I take to be the most important divine attributes of the deistic God for the purposes of this project. In the following section I discuss omniscience, timelessness, immutability, and necessity, as these are some of the divine attributes that do not seem as crucial to the overall deistic conception as those discussed in the previous two sections but still need to be addressed in a discussion such as this. The final substantive section of the chapter, *The Role That These Attributes Play in Deism*, discusses how each of the particular interpretations of the divine attributes discussed up to that point ultimately factor into the overall conception of the deistic God that I present and argue for.

Chapter 5 is divided into two parts. In the first three sections I discuss the teleological argument, the ontological argument, and the cosmological argument to show how a deistic conception of God is compatible with these common arguments for the existence of God. In the second part of the chapter, the following three sections, I discuss the problem of divine hiddenness, the problem of evil, and the problems with miracles as several of the stronger and more well-known contemporary arguments against God's existence that generally pose challenges for the classical theistic conception of God. Finally, I discuss how a deistic conception of God may be able to get around some of the difficulties that classical theism faces in dealing with these arguments.

In chapter 6 I present a possible alternative to the kind of deism that I propose. This alternative is called noninterventionist special divine action, but I refer to it as epistemic deism and go on to explain why such a change in terminology is warranted. I detail the nature of three different noninterventionist special divine action theories, as presented by Nancey Murphy, Thomas Tracy, and Bradley Monton, and I discuss why and how each of these three theories can all be reduced to epistemic deism. I go on to describe how epistemic deism as a whole is ultimately an unviable ontological view and why it is substantially inferior to the kind of deism that I argue for in this project.

In chapter 7, I discuss some potential difficulties and further lines of thought that the multiverse deist will need to address at some point, but that are ultimately not within the scope of this project. I begin by revisiting several difficulties for the theist in accepting a multiverse theory without accepting deism that were discussed in chapter 3. Moving through the remainder of the chapter there are discussions of difficulties that may arise for the multiverse deist from explaining a deistic God's role in creation of the universe, the need to determine the location of a deistic God within the multiverse, the need to abandon the idea of a personal relationship with God as the greatest possible good, reconciling the idea of a non-active God with the biblical accounts of an active God and, finally, accounting for the various miracles and religious experiences that have been reported throughout history. The aim of this chapter is only to draw attention to some of the other lines of research that can be pursued as a result of the work that has been done in this project to this point.

Finally, in chapter 8, as the title suggests, I address several of the practical and considerations and venture my concluding thoughts of the overall project. Here I note that there are still many serious questions that will need to be answered if there is hope to construct a full-fledged worldview. While these remaining questions and lines of thought are, by no means, easy to provide answers to, I remain optimistic that, at the very least, meaningful discussion can come from them.

In conceiving of and completing this project, while I made several arguments for the existence of a deistic God and for some particular interpretations of His[2] nature, the overall goal is simply to open the discussion of, what I feel is, an under-discussed ontological view. Coming into this project I felt that deism could have been a plausible ontological view with some potential upsides and, in moving through my research, I think that I have not only confirmed that feeling but also pointed out precisely why it is plausible, where the upsides to deism are and bring to light some areas where it is potentially weak as an overall view. My hope is that, in bringing up this under-discussed topic of deism and discussing it in relation to the multiverse, which is one of the most active areas in the philosophy of religion today, I can rekindle some interest in this ontological view as a plausible alternative to classical theism. This work will, hopefully, serve as the starting point for much more research and discussion on deism, either as it relates to the multiverse or as a standalone ontological view.

NOTES

1. As is evidenced and noted by Buckareff & Nagasawa (2016).

2. I use the pronouns "He/Him/His" when referring to God because these are the pronouns that have typically been used to refer to God in historical, Western, analytic philosophy of religion and also in scripture. While I utilize these pronouns for reasons of personal comfort and consistency this, in no way, forces the presupposition that God is gendered in any way. These pronouns simply serve as placeholders that can be replaced by any other pronouns that the reader deems more appropriate.

Chapter 2

The Case for the Multiverse

In the past several decades there has been an increasing amount of work done, both by philosophers and by scientists, addressing multiverse theories and their relevant hypotheses. From the philosophical side, multiverse theories have been motivated by a variety of factors, they have been argued for in various ways, and they have come in a variety of structures. Be they independently motivated, put forth by theists as a response to particular arguments for atheism, or put forth by atheists as an objection against particular arguments for theism, and whether the multiverses that they discuss comprise an infinite number of spatiotemporally disconnected universes, a finite number of spatiotemporally disconnected universes, or have any other kind of composition, a significant number and variety of multiverse theories have been discussed by and among thinkers. Because of the number of varying and divergent multiverse accounts that have been, and are currently being, discussed, even if we grant that a multiverse exists, there is still an equally large amount of competing views regarding the nature of the possible universes that are supposed to populate this multiverse. Of course, when discussing something of this nature, precisely what "possible" means is a crucial question that must be answered, and one that can spawn an entirely separate discussion altogether.

Just as the discussion of multiverses has gone on in the philosophical world, so too has the discussion in the scientific world. Scientists from various disciplines have carried out work in the attempt to determine the plausibility of different structures and compositions of competing multiverse theories. Similar to the models and compositions discussed by philosophers that are alluded to above, scientific models have been set to determine many aspects of the multiverse discussion, as well. Scientists now engage themselves in providing answers for what could have been before the Big Bang, what will happen if and when our current universe ceases to exist, whether it is even really possible to conceptualize and construct a multiverse, what the existence of a multiverse would mean for us in this particular universe, what the possible compositions and physical constants of other universes may be, and the like.

As I have put it thus far, I may have given the impression that there is a clear divide between the work of philosophers and the work of scientists when it comes to exploration of multiverse theories, but this is not the case. Philosophical work on the multiverse and scientific work on the multiverse are not mutually exclusive and the two can and often do influence one another, with each side borrowing and implementing information from the other, blurring the lines between the two disciplines. While the two sides are looking at the same ideas, it is the methodologies by which they go about exploring these ideas that differentiate the two from one another. So while philosophy, at one extreme of the spectrum, may be limited to making theoretical cases for a multiverse via inductive or deductive reasoning using a variety of previous knowledge, assumptions and postulations, physicists, at the other end of the spectrum, have the ability to engage in actual experimentation and field studies to ascertain answers to questions about the plausibility and nature of different multiverse theories. Of course, as this is on a continuum, in the middle, we will find differing accounts that appeal to varying degrees of hard science and philosophical outlooks, blending the two together. The philosophy of science, and the philosophy of math, for example, both lie closer to the middle of the continuum and can contribute to the multiverse debate through the philosophical examination of different principles of science and math that are being used by the scientists in their approaches.[1]

This particular chapter aims to do several things, all primarily in the way of setting the stage and providing a bit of context for what will come to be discussed in further chapters. In the first section, I discuss the philosophical case being made for a multiverse. I discuss several of the predominant multiverse views and their motivations, outlining the methodology and structure behind these multiverse theories. In the following section, I do the same for scientific approaches to the multiverse. This section, again, discusses the methodologies and structures of various proposed multiverse models, but this time from the scientific perspective. These two presentations, however, do not provide an evaluation of any of the theories proposed; instead they will serve to bring some of the recent and predominant work on the multiverse to your attention. Of course, the degree of plausibility of the competing multiverse accounts vary slightly, or perhaps even considerably, but that is not of prime importance in this case. What is important is the plausibility and worthwhileness of the multiverse discussion in its entirety. Finally, I discuss the multiverse pursuit as a whole, and its overall plausibility given both philosophical and scientific approaches. While my aim in this section is not to confirm or disconfirm the veridicality of the arguments for the existence of a multiverse, it is to show that the exploration of the discussion as a whole is fruitful and that it is worth continuing and advancing regardless of whether or not you subscribe to a particular multiverse account.

THE PHILOSOPHICAL CASE FOR THE MULTIVERSE

The role of this section is to serve as an introduction to some of the prevailing views in the world of multiverse-thought, outlining several of the predominant and well-known philosophical arguments for the multiverse. This is not intended to serve as a full-fledged survey chapter, as other substantial survey papers and edited volumes on the multiverse have already been written by others.[2] Furthermore, the limitation of my discussion of various philosophical views is due to the fact that any broader exploration of competing viewpoints is simply irrelevant to the overall aim of this section, which can be achieved through the discussion of just several accounts. The aim here is to provide a brief introduction to the variety of multiverse theories that exist within philosophy and to demonstrate that there is no single model to which the philosophical community as a whole subscribes. The variety of multiverse accounts present within philosophical discourse leads me to two conclusions: (1) that there are a number of highly intelligent academics working on different aspects of these ideas so we ought to afford, at least the initial idea of a multiverse, a certain level of plausibility and worthwhileness[3] and (2) that the sheer number of different accounts means that there is more likely to be one that strikes the reader as more plausible than others, meaning that even in the case that the reader rejects the vast majority of philosophical multiverse accounts there still exists the possibility that he finds one as plausible and subscribes to it.[4] Now, let us move on to the discussion of some of the philosophical views.

Motivated to respond to the argument from evil, Jason Megill puts forward his account for the plausibility of a multiverse (Megill, 2001). While he does not explicitly outline exactly just what his multiverse would look like (i.e., how it would be formed, what it would consist of, etc.) he provides reasons for believing that a multiverse may exist, regardless of the particular composition-brand one may subscribe to. That is to say, the reasons that he provides are consistent with a variety of different multiverse compositions. The sole detail regarding any attribute of the multiverse discussed is the possibility of a threshold of inclusion that suggests that only universes that contain more good than evil will be created by God and thus will be the only universes contained within the multiverse. While he does not argue explicitly that this is the required threshold, it remains his sole discussion of and suggestion for what may constitute the composition of the multiverse (Megill, 2011, p. 133). Megill goes on to allude to several different scientific views about the multiverse, both to act as evidence for his claim that belief in the multiverse is a plausible position to accept and to demonstrate that, even within the scientific community, there is no single viewpoint on just what a multiverse may look like.[5] Megill gives five reasons for the acceptance of the plausibility of the multiverse: (1) that his premise that a multiverse is possible is so weak that it is plausible, (2) that it has not been conclusively shown that a multiverse does not exist, leaving it epistemically possible that there is one, (3) that it is entailed by several current theories in physics, (4) given that it is entailed by current theories in physics it cannot be denied by some of the most likely opponents, and (5) that denial of the multiverse theory would strengthen the theist's position by leaving God's creative act as the only possible explanation for the fine-tuning, thus making such a denial imprudent for the atheist (Megill, 2011, p. 131).

While the structure and overall argument forwarded by Megill differs, both in its motivation and in the kind of multiverse that it proposes, from the argument presented by Donald Turner (Turner, 2004) the two appear to share some common ground. Much like Megill, Turner argues for a multiverse[6] that is composed only of universes[7] with a "preponderance of good over evil" (Turner, 2004, p. 158). So, while Turner acknowledges the possibility of a multiverse containing every logically possible universe, he argues that if his account is to stand up to the problem of evil, then the threshold below which God chooses not to create any universes is the balance between good and evil. That is to say, on Turner's account, no individual universe will contain more evil than good, and thus no universe in the multiverse will be on-balance bad.

A further alternative viewpoint on the multiverse is presented by Hud Hudson who suggests, rather than the series of spatiotemporally isolated universes that are typically proposed in multiverse theories, what he calls a hyperspace (Hudson, 2005). Hudson's hyperspace is essentially an additional dimension to the three dimensions of time-space that we are accustomed to. Hudson describes his hypothesis of a plenitudinous hyperspace by saying that "spacetime is a connected manifold with more than three spatial dimensions, yet the manifold can be partitioned into subregions which vary independently with respect to their cosmic conditions" (Hudson, 2005, p. 40). So while the language used to describe Hudson's hyperspace varies from the language of other multiverse theories, the product still seems to be quite similar: a series of universes, or regions, that exhaust a wide variety of cosmic conditions. In discussing his hyperspace model in relation to the fine-tuning argument, Hudson says the following:

[G]iven the fine-tuning, the hypothesis of a plenitudinous hyperspace should of itself lead us to very high expectations that the cosmic conditions will be life-permitting. Why? Presumably because, on the assumption of a sufficiently rich plenitude, there will be enough distinct regions in which the physical parameters differ independently to render it unsurprising that at least some of them fall in the life-permitting range. (Hudson, 2005, pp. 41–42)

So while this is a specific discussion of hyperspace that is preferential to a three-dimensional conception of time-space in relation to the fine-tuning argument, it does a good job in illustrating the composition of Hudson's account. The two prime elements that differentiate Hudson's account from others seem to be that, first, Hudson's account speaks of different regions being found in different dimensions of space-time rather than merely different universes being found in different spatial or temporal locations that other multiverse accounts appeal to.[8] In having a series of different universes existing at different space or time locations there does not appear to be any need to invoke an extra dimension of space-time to accommodate for the existence of other universes, but this is not the case for the hyperspace account. And secondly, while many other multiverse accounts often maintain that different universes within the multiverse are spatiotemporally isolated from one another, it is not the case that the same isolation is necessary or present between regions in Hudson's account, in that it seems to leave open the possibility of accessing one dimension from another dimension or of accessing one region from another region. Of course, the practical implications of crossing such dimensional or regional lines is an entirely different discussion but, that aside, there does not seem to be anything inherent in the hyperspace account that precludes such a traversal.

Coming from different motivations, Klaas Kraay proposes a unique multiverse account that he sees as a response to the "best possible worlds" objection to theism (Kraay, 2010). Kraay argues that the best possible world need not be equated to a single universe and that the best possible world can actually be a set (possibly an extremely large or infinite set) of universes. Given the nature of God, an unsurpassably good being, He would create all of the universes that are worth creating (Kraay, 2010, p. 360). That is to say; given some vague threshold of goodness that determines whether a particular universe is worthy or unworthy of God's creation and sustenance, for any universe above that threshold, God would create and sustain it. The total collection of all of these universes that are worthy of creation and sustenance would then collectively comprise our world. A world which contains a number of worthy, spatiotemporally disconnected universes. Kraay calls this the "Theistic Multiverse" (TM), and in TM, "God creates and sustains *all* and *only* those universes which are worth creating" (Kraay, 2010, p. 363). Because of the nature of God and the structure of this world, Kraay concludes that if one accepts various principles that he has put forth[9] "are plausible, and if TM is logically possible, the theist must maintain that the actual world is TM, and that it is the unique best of all divinely actualisable worlds" (Kraay, 2010, pp. 364–65). So on this account, Kraay argues not only that a multiverse is a logically possible world but that the theist ought to accept that it is the actual world, and subsequently that it is the only possible world, simultaneously rendering it the best possible world.

The final account to be discussed in this section is one that I am currently developing and it hinges on the nature of the relationship between God and free will. If it is plausible that free will is the greatest possible good,[10] and God is all-loving and perfectly good,[11] then it seems that God would be required to maximize the amount of free will in the universe.[12] Since free will is not something that can be measured qualitatively, since my free will cannot be *better* than your free will, it must be measured quantitatively. That is to say, for God to maximize the amount of free will in the universe, He must quantitatively maximize the number of instances that free agents exercise their free will. Imagine that each free choice made by each individual in our universe counts as one unit of good. So, my choosing to have granola for breakfast is one unit of good, my choosing to put strawberry yogurt on that granola is a unit of good, my choosing to eat my granola and yogurt from a particular bowl is a unit of good.[13] Similarly, I could have chosen to have oatmeal for breakfast, I could have chosen to put brown sugar on my oatmeal, and I could have chosen to eat it straight from the pot in which I made it. Supposing that these two different breakfast scenarios are mutually exclusive and the only options available, I could have only actualized three of six decisions, and thus only garnered three units of good while leaving three units of good untouched. In order to create a maximally good universe, however, God must have it so that no units of good are left untouched. For this to happen, another universe in which I decide to eat brown sugar oatmeal out of a pot for breakfast must be actualized somewhere. For this particular example, the existence of these two universes would exhaust the number of free choices available, thus maximizing the number of units of good that are enjoyed between the two, which creates a maximally good multiverse.

Of course, the example just presented is exceptionally simplistic and limited in scope, but is introduced merely to illustrate how this multiverse model works at its most basic level. We could imagine a similar situation in which eating Froot Loops, eating a bagel, and not eating breakfast at all are all available free choices and that for each one of these options there is an actual universe where it is actualized. Similarly, this process would be carried out for each free choice made throughout the lifetime of each individual agent, and so too would each possible collective conjunction of free choices between other free agents. This would result in an enormously large number of distinct universes that ultimately exhaust every possible free choice and combination of free choices, leading to a multiverse that has realized the greatest possible number of units of good (as they relate to free choice). A multiverse that realizes every potential unit of good is a maximally good universe, one that a perfectly good and all-loving God would be compelled, or perhaps even required, to create.

Some may argue that even if God is required to create a maximally good universe and, even if it is also true that free will is the greatest possible good, we need not appeal to a multiverse model to reconcile the two. We could simply imagine one universe in which there are enough free agents actualizing enough free choices in order to exhaust and gain all possible units of good. Surely this would create a maximally good universe without the use of a multiverse. In response to an objection such as this, while there is no doubt that a single-universe model such as this would yield a *good* universe, perhaps one that satisfies proponents of a "threshold" model of greatest possible worlds, I am after a maximally good ontological view, and a single universe just cannot satisfy that since I would leave too many goods as potential rather than actual.

Another reason that a single-universe model would not satisfy the kind of maximal good that I am after is that no matter how good a particular universe may be, enjoying an enormously large number of agents who make a variety of free choices, such a universe could always be improved upon with the addition of one more freely acting agent. The addition of one more agent would result in, minimally, one more free choice being made by that agent, increasing the overall goodness of that universe. For any single-universe model, no matter how many agents there are, there could always be one more added to increase the goodness of that universe, and yet even with that addition of any arbitrary number of agents there would still be a multitude of unclaimed units of good because of the inability to actualize each possible free choice. The same cannot be said of the multiverse model outlined above since it, by its very nature, exhausts all possibilities of free choices as well as all possible combinations of free choices. So, yes, for any individual universe within the multiverse one more agent could be added to create a universe with more good in it, but such a universe already exists elsewhere in the multiverse. Having the existence of such a universe (with that added agent in it) means that the goodness is merely realized in another universe, yet still within the same multiverse, which is the scope on which the maximal goodness of concern ought to be measured.

For those who find it difficult to maintain that free will is the greatest possible good there are still several possible alternatives that could yield the existence of a multiverse. In the first alternative, it seems that we can substitute something such as happiness, joy, or pleasure for free will, and the multiverse account may still remain the same. Surely we can agree that there are different types of happiness, and failing that; there are at least different ways of attaining happiness.[14] This being the case there would seem to be different kinds of happiness that are incompatible with each other, such as the happiness or satisfaction felt from eating the last piece of your favorite cake immediately, and the happiness or satisfaction felt from saving that same piece of your favorite cake for later and enjoying it after a period of anticipation. Assuming that the situations that we are talking about both involve the exact same person and the exact same piece of cake then it seems that enjoying both of these kinds of happiness is not possible since one cannot both be happy that he is currently enjoying the last piece of his favorite cake while simultaneously enjoying the anticipation of being able to enjoy his favorite piece of cake at a later time. Returning to the previous terminology of "units of good," with each kind of happiness equating to one unit of good, then, in this case, only one unit of good could be recognized while the other is left as potential. In order to recognize both units of good and create a maximally good world (or multiverse), a second universe would be needed so that both kinds of happiness can be instantiated.

The same principle follows for a wide range of other goods such as for example, justice, existence, life, and so on. For each different good, it seems that within it there are multiple variations of that good that may not be compatible with each other, thus requiring a multiverse in order to realize all of them. While I will not go on into such detail as to provide examples, as I have done with free will and happiness, it stands that such an account is at least plausible and that for any good that is argued to be the greatest possible good a multiverse will be entailed by it.

Secondly, for those who do not want to maintain that there is a single greatest possible good, rather that there are a variety of inherent goods that are on-par with one another or that there is a greater goodness held in a variety of goods rather than a flood of one greatest possible good, this too could entail a multiverse. In this case, it is not altogether clear that there is a single instantiation of a variety of goods is any better than any other instantiation, and given the principle of plenitude, it still seems that God would create a multiverse in order to realize all possible combinations of goods. For example, it is not clear that a universe, universe A, whose maximal goodness is composed of 50 percent happiness, 30 percent justice and 20 percent free will is any better than another universe, universe B, whose maximal goodness is composed of 40 percent life, 25 percent pleasure and 35 percent honesty. Whether universe A is better than universe B or not, it seems that God would be obliged to create both of these universes, and a whole host more, since they are all on-balance good, and more of a good thing is a better thing. The universes that God would create would be ones that exhaust every possible composition of every inherent good that yields an on-balance good universe, thus resulting in a maximally good multiverse. Again, while the individual universes themselves will not yield maximal goodness, they comprise a multiverse that is maximally good.

THE SCIENTIFIC CASE FOR THE MULTIVERSE

As with the case in philosophy, much work is going on in the sciences (primarily physics, for our purposes) regarding multiverse theories. Tim Wilkinson notes that "[a]t the coal force of science . . . it is usually extra-ordinarily difficult to find even one theory that fits the facts. In the current context, we do have a few competing theories, but all imply broadly the same thing: a multiverse" (2013, p. 94), meaning that while a survey of the literature seems to suggest that there is scientific consensus on the existence of a multiverse the debate arises in just what *kind* of multiverse we happen to be a part of. For the scientific community, according to Wilkinson, the question is not *whether* a multiverse exists, rather there are questions about the composition of the multiverse, the origins, the physical constants of the multiverse and the individual universes within it, and so on. Similar to the previous section and the treatment of philosophical discussions of the multiverse the following is a short introduction to several ideas within physics regarding the multiverse.[15] While I do not generally go into detail regarding the methodology and justification for the various multiverse accounts presented (since they are typically quite complex and laden with mathematical jargon) I present the concluding prediction of each theory. The reason for including a section on the scientific perspectives of the multiverse, in this overall philosophical discussion, is twofold. In the first case, scientific approaches to the multiverse provide us with just that, a different approach, bringing to light different conceptions of the composition, formation, and general structure and nature of the multiverse. The second reason is that, while philosophical approaches to the multiverse may be logically consistent and conceivable, scientific approaches seem to have that extra level of justification given that they have to be not only logically consistent but physically plausible as well. That is to say; I think that any philosophical view of the multiverse, no matter how strong it may be, can be strengthened and given more credibility if it is supported by a scientific account of the multiverse.

Max Tegmark composed a paper that serves as somewhat of a survey paper, not of particular scientific theories of the multiverse, but of the different and more general types of multiverse theories available within physics (Tegmark, 2007). Tegmark argues that most (if not all) current scientific multiverse theories taken seriously propose or predict multiverses that fit into one of four distinct categories, or *levels*, as he calls them. Each level, beginning with level 1, progressively varies more and more (with regards to the physical constants, laws of nature, etc.) from our universe. Similarly, as the levels progress up from 1 to 4 the multiverse theories that fall under them become increasingly debated and less easily accepted. That is to say, level one is the multiverse model that contains individual universes that are most similar to ours, and is also the multiverse model that garners the fewest objections and sparks the least debate within the scientific community whereas the level 4 multiverse is the model that contains individual universes that vary significantly from ours and is also the multiverse model that is met with the highest levels of skepticism.

Tegmark's level 1 multiverse is a series of parallel universes that maintain the same (or at least very similar) physical constants as our universe but realize all initial conditions. That is to say, all possible realities, given our physical constants, are actualized in some other parallel universe. A universe in a multiverse such as this would look very similar to the one that we are currently in, save for different initial starting conditions. So, for example, while another universe would enjoy remarkably similar physical constants and laws of nature as ours, it would have a different initial starting point, making it, perhaps, at a point in development 2,000 years behind our universe, or perhaps 2,000 years ahead of our universe. The universes within this multiverse are inaccessible to other universes, and due to the rate of expansion and the distance between the universes, it would not be possible, says Tegmark, for one to ever travel between universes.

The level 2 multiverse is essentially composed of an "infinite set of distinct Level 1 Multiverses, each represented by a bubble . . . some perhaps with different dimensionality and different physical constants" (Tegmark, 2007, p. 105). Each bubble contains a distinct parallel universe that displays not only initial conditions different from those of the next bubble but also different physical constants and laws of nature (Tegmark, 2007, p. 107). So this second level is similar to the first in its makeup, the difference coming in the potential variations of physical constants and laws of nature. On this level it simply seems that there is the possibility of a greater number of universes than on level one, since there is a broader range in which the physical constants of each universe can fall, thus yielding more possibilities and more universes. Also differentiating this level from level 1 is that, on this level, all universes appear to exist simultaneously, which is a detail that does not seem necessary on level 1.

Tegmark's level 3 multiverse, I think, is better understood in relation to the first two levels rather than through pure explication of it. The level 3 multiverse, while it adds no new storylines beyond levels 1 or 2, varies in how these storylines come to be. Whereas in level 1 and 2 the universes are far apart, in level 3 they are all spatially very close, so to speak. This is because rather than being a series of disconnected independent universes in the levels previously discussed, on this level the universes are merely different branches of the same tree. Tegmark does not explicitly describe whether or not these different branches are able to interact with each other causally, and I would expect him to say that they do not, but that they are still interconnected in some sense. On levels 1 and 2, we can think of our counterpart selves doing other than we are doing here in some distant universe, whereas on level 3 our counterpart merely is on another "quantum branch in infinite-dimensional Hilbert space" unknown to us simply by our epistemic limitations (Tegmark, 2007, pp. 112–13), and this seems to indicate that these different branches may be connected yet causally isolated from one another.

Finally, the level 4 multiverse "involves the idea of mathematical democracy, in which universes governed by other equations are equally real. This implies the notion that a mathematical structure and the physical world are in some sense identical. It also means that mathematical structures are 'out there,' in the sense that mathematicians discover them rather than create them" (Tegmark, 2007, p. 116). This seems to entail a variety of universes that are widely divergent from the one that we are currently in, resulting in a seemingly infinite amount of universes that would be unrecognizable to us. The universes in the level 4 multiverse contain "different fundamental physical laws" (Tegmark, 2007, p. 121), which means that the range of individual universes that we could see on this level far surpasses the range of universes that we could see in levels 1–3. Not only would we be able to have all possible storylines be realized, as is the case for levels 1–3, but we would be able to see all possible storylines that are compatible with each possible set of fundamental physical laws.

So, while Tegmark does not exactly propose any new scientific account of the multiverse, what he does do is set up a framework by which we can differentiate and classify existing or future scientific multiverse accounts. Tegmark's levels of classification allow us to see just how far particular multiverse theories range from what we know about, and see within, our own universe, as well as allow us to see how multiverse theories vary from one other in terms of what they call for with regard to physical constants of the universes that they contain.

The second scientific approach to the multiverse that will be discussed is one similar to Tegmark's level 3 multiverse discussed above and is proposed as an answer to the problem that the "Schrödinger's Cat" thought experiment posed for what we can claim about our knowledge of the physical world (Norris, 1999). This particular account was put forth by David Deutsch (1997), and subsequently discussed by Christopher Norris. Of Deutsch's account, Norris says

On this account—in brief—*every possible* outcome of *every* wavepacket collapse is *simultaneously and actually realized* through constant branching of alternative quantum worlds that are all of them equally "real" though only one of them is epistemically accessible to any individual observer at any particular time. For the observer must likewise be thought of as having previously split into a whole multitude of observers, each of them consciously inhabiting a "world" whose history is itself just one among the manifold world-versions that have eventuated up to the point through the exfoliating series of wavepacket collapses. Thus he or she will have any number of counterpart "selves" distributed across those worlds and each possessing a lifeline which, if traced back far enough, will rejoin his/her own at some crucial point just before their paths forked off into henceforth divergent and non-communicating series. (Norris, 1999, pp. 312–13)

Furthermore, Deutsch does not want to limit these other worlds to maintaining our physical constants or laws of nature. While it is not explicitly stated just how far the laws of nature and physical constants of these other worlds or universes may vary from those in ours, I think that it would be safe to say that Deutsch may have in mind the kinds of variations found in Tegmark's level 3 and 4 multiverses. In short, Deutsch's account says that we need to adopt "the multiverse theory and assuming that *all* possibilities have been realized in one or another of the multiple worlds that diverge at every point where some particular world-specific event . . . happens to occur" (Norris, 1999, p. 314). Of course, just what exactly constitutes a possibility for Deutsch depends highly on his range of allowable divergence between the physical constants of our universe and those of other universes, but the principle still remains regardless of the lack of an explicit explanation.

The final scientific account to be mentioned here is that of A. D. Linde, who argues for a kind of self-reproducing multiverse (Linde, 1987). This brand of multiverse account can be seen as one in which not all universes contained within the multiverse are actualized or exist simultaneously, rather they all come to exist (generally one-by-one) over a period of time. Linde's account, argues, in particular, that "the large-scale quantum fluctuations of the scalar field . . . generated in the chaotic inflation scenario lead to an infinite process of self-reproduction of inflationary mini-universes."[16] He suggests a "model of an eternally existing chaotic inflationary universe."[17] Linde goes on to cite scientific and mathematical reasons for how this particular multiverse model is predicted. Of this prediction, Linde explains that

In our case the universe infinitely regenerates itself, and there is no global "end of time." Moreover, it is not necessary to assume that the universe as a whole was created at some initial moment. . . . The process of creation of each new mini-universe . . . occurs independently of the pre-history of the universe. . . .

Therefore the whole process can be considered as an infinite chain reaction of creation and self-reproduction which has no end and which may have no beginning. (Linde, 1987, pp. 172–73)

So, in this case, the universe goes on regenerating itself eternally with, in theory, every possible universe instantiation eventually being realized at one point or another within this string of eternally self-reproducing universes. While Linde does not specify the exact process through which these individual universes come to pass in and out of existence (their lifespan, so to speak), he does make several suggestions that allow him to show that his model is consistent with various competing scientific theories regarding exactly just how such a process may be feasible.

THE INTERSECTION BETWEEN SCIENTIFIC AND PHILOSOPHICAL APPROACHES TO THE MULTIVERSE

As I have presented it, it may seem as if scientists and philosophers are working independently and in isolation of one another on matters of the multiverse, but this is not the case. Increasingly, philosophers are adopting and importing scientific work into their theories to both guide the arguments that they initially set out to make and serve as important tangible evidence for the cases that they go on to make. It is no longer the case that multiverse theories are relegated to pure speculation and loose inductive reasoning, instead now philosophers have substantial evidence from the scientific community to support their views regarding the nature of our existence, something that was once a far loftier ambition. That is not to say, of course, that the scientific views employed by philosophers are without controversy themselves. Just as various philosophical views face rival theories and conceptions, as we have just seen, so too do the scientific theories. We have just noted several different kinds of scientific theories that conclude in widely divergent types of multiverses, assuredly with each one being argued for by many experts in the field while simultaneously being argued against by many experts in the field. Scientific approaches to the multiverse will also sometimes borrow ideas from philosophical explorations, using various philosophical models to craft their hypotheses in the initial stages of experimentation to explore the possibilities and entailments of a multiverse. It is not often the case that experiments of this sort will begin with no aim; instead, there must be an idea present, something that is being searched for, an inquiry for which some answer is sought. These foundational inquiries are the things that philosophy can and does supply for the scientific world. Those aforementioned lofty philosophical projects serve as initial starting points for mathematicians, physicists and other scientists to begin their work, to aim to confirm or disconfirm some idea or thought. This is the role that philosophy plays in the science of the multiverse.

One of the more significant questions or obstacles to be dealt with when dealing with navigating between scientific and philosophical discussions of the multiverse, or in any discussion of the multiverse for that matter, is the task of figuring out whether or not the various sides of the discussion are even talking about the same thing.[18] There are two critical distinctions between scientific accounts of the multiverse and philosophical accounts of the multiverse that will need to be clarified before any meaningful discussion can go on between the two. The first distinction to be made, one which contains a wide variety of further distinctions that must be made within it, is that of semantics. The multiverse discussion, unlike some other philosophical or scientific discussions, does not yet seem to have within it a precise and commonly accepted set of terms that carry with them exact definitions of how they ought to be used in various contexts. One of the most common cases of this is distinguishing between terms such as "universe" and "world," with Tim Wilkinson noting that "[c]onfusingly, philosophers and physicists use 'possible worlds' and 'possible universes' interchangeably" (2013, p. 89). In some cases "universe" is taken to mean, and is used to refer to, the totality of all things in existence. That is to say; nothing can exist outside of the universe (except perhaps God, on some accounts, but this is not important for our purposes quite yet).[19] In some cases with this usage of "universe," "worlds" are considered to be smaller self-contained, often disconnected, sections within the "universe." Each "world," in this case, would exemplify a different way that things could have been, and collectively all of the "worlds" would compose the larger "universe." On other accounts, it is the exact opposite, with the "world" being taken as the term to connote the totality of existence and a variety of "universes" that make up this world. With this in mind, it is not always altogether clear just how to compare and discuss various multiverse accounts that, while they may be using the same terms, will suffer from semantic incongruence. Similarly, various scientists and philosophers will coin their own terms to describe different levels of encompassment of the "worlds" or "universes" that they aim to discuss, so these too must be navigated and, in a sense, translated to undertake an accurate comparison among other accounts. Moving forward, the way that I will employ these terms will be as follows. When I speak of a multiverse, I am referring to a collection of universes (at least two) that, together, comprise the totality of all that is in existence. When I speak of universes, I am referring to spatiotemporally and causally disconnected units that comprise the multiverse. Universes are entirely self-contained and, for those beings and objects existing within their respective universes, represent the confines in which all causal relations can take place. And finally, when I speak of a world, I am referring to the totality of all that is in existence. In some cases, this will equate to a universe, and in some cases, it will equate to a multiverse, and this will vary depending on the particular ontological view being discussed. For a single-universe model, the world will consist of that single universe, whereas on a multiverse model the world will consist of all of the universes that form the multiverse.

Somewhat tied in with issues of semantics, and a potential influence of the differences that we see within the terminology of the discussion, are the motivations from which philosophical accounts and scientific accounts of the multiverse stem. On the one hand, scientific approaches to the multiverse are often concerned with justifying or delving into accounts of how the various universes that comprise the multiverse can come to pass in and out of existence. That is to say; scientific accounts are generally concerned with exploring the physical constants, laws of nature, mathematical structures, and the like, of these possible universes to determine whether or not their existence is even physically possible. Building on whether these individual universes are physically possible or not, the scientific approach will also go on to investigate by what process it is possible that these universes come into existence, what relation they may have to one another, whether or not it is possible that multiple universes exist at the same time, whether or not it is plausible for them to fit together into a multiverse, what the structure of this multiverse would be, and so forth. Scientists are generally concerned less with the contents of various universes than they are with the structure of the multiverse as a whole. They tend to focus purely on the aspects concerning the physical plausibility of different multiverse models.

Philosophical accounts of the multiverse not only concern themselves with different aspects of the multiverse than do scientific accounts but also begin with and are often motivated by very different goals. Philosophical multiverse accounts often tend to be driven by a desire to respond to various atheistic arguments. Philosophers can appeal to multiverse accounts in attempts to block various arguments for atheism, with these arguments for atheism generally being some version of the problem of evil or the problem of no-best-world. On the other hand, philosophers may also appeal to multiverse theories to undercut theistic arguments for God's existence, namely, the fine-tuning argument. Given these motivations, the philosophical multiverse account is generally concerned not so much with determining how the universe came to be, as the scientific account is; instead it is more concerned with evaluating the overall value of various aspects of the multiverse. That is to say, evaluating the overall value of particular universes within the multiverse, or the multiverse as a whole, and determining whether or not certain universes ought to be considered as worthy of being part of the multiverse, or at least as being possible parts of it. It should be noted that the common employment of multiverse theories by the philosopher as a response to some objection can be seen as detrimental to itself, in some cases, with some philosophers seeing the multiverse theory as an *ad hoc* response to some particular argument. And that seems to be one of the more significant differences between scientific and philosophical multiverse accounts. While philosophical accounts are often mounted as a theistic response to deal with some particular atheistic objection to the existence of God (or as an atheistic response to some theistic argument for the existence of God), scientific accounts generally appear to be more independently motivated.

CONCLUSION

In this chapter, we have seen the differences between several philosophical multiverse accounts, as well as the differences between several different scientific multiverse accounts. Furthermore, we have seen that, while philosophical and scientific multiverse theories may come from different motivations and argue for different kinds of multiverses, the two disciplines do not operate independently of one another, with each side often taking and employing information and ideas from the other for their own theories. The result of this information and idea-sharing is a wide range of divergent multiverse theories, varying in terms of composition, value, makeup and origins, among other things.

Overall, this chapter aimed to present an overview of some of the prevailing multiverse views at work today and to demonstrate not only that there is a broad range of ideas at play but also that these views ought to be given serious consideration when considering the adoption of an ontological view.

NOTES

1. One particular area where this can be seen is in the discussion of actual infinites, which can be applied to whether or not a multiverse can contain an infinite number of universes rather than merely an extremely large finite number of universes. Some examples of work on infinites can be seen in Shapiro (2011), Tapp (2011), and Gabriele (2012).

2. For more in-depth survey pieces or additional discussions and accounts of the philosophical multiverse see Kraay (2012; 2015), Stewart (1993), Draper (2004), Forrest (1996), O'Connor (2008), Parfit (1998), and McHarry (1978).

3. I understand that this may appear to be an appeal to authority, but I make no claim regarding the acceptance of any claims regarding the multiverse. I merely want to point out that there is a substantial amount of serious work being done in the area

and that, given that, we should not completely dismiss the idea of a multiverse as entirely implausible and outlandish as some might be tempted to do.

4. Some strategic credit here is owed to St. Thomas Aquinas and his presentation of the Five Ways.

5. See Vaidman (2008), Section 1, Tegmark (2003), Jacobs (2009), Section 2a for more detailed discussion.

6. Which he calls a *cosmos*.

7. Which he calls *simple universes*.

8. While his discussion is typically confined to discussion of the fourth dimension of time-space, it is compatible with any larger finite number of space-time dimensions.

9. See Kraay (2010), Section 4.

10. This is essentially taken as an extension of free will theodicy which argues that free will is a higher-level good, but I go the extra step in asserting that it could be the greatest possible good. See Plantinga (1965).

11. As it is in the case of the classical God of Judeo-Christian monotheism.

12. In just the same way as a utilitarian is required to maximize utility.

13. It can generally be argued that the kinds of free choices that free will theodicy values are those that are morally significant, but I make or require no such distinction here.

14. For the sake of simplicity, I will refer to each of these as simply being a different "kind" of happiness.

15. For additional scientific perspectives on the multiverse see Smolin (1997), Steinhardt & Turok (2007), Wallace (2012), Linde (2000), Veneziano (2006), Ellis (2011), and Carr (2007).

16. See Linde (1987), Abstract.

17. See Linde (1987), Abstract.

18. This is also touched on by Kraay (2010, pp. 359–60).

19. This will be discussed in chapter 7.

Chapter 3

The Theist and the Multiverse

As we have seen, the case that is being made for multiverse theories is in full-force from a variety of different perspectives and motivations and also seems to have a level of credibility and plausibility backing it. Coming from both the philosophical arguments and the scientific experimentation and research it appears that there is a solid case for the existence or, minimally, the plausibility of a multiverse with the only questions remaining relating to the particular construct of multiverse of which we happen to be a part. It seems that this being the case, theists could reasonably be willing to accept the existence of a multiverse as an ontological view. But if this is to happen, what exactly does it mean for the theist? Does adopting such an ontological view harm or hurt him in any way? Is it compatible with his theological beliefs? What are the potential drawbacks for a theist in adopting a multiverse view? These are some of the questions that any theist would have to consider before the adoption of a multiverse account in favor of a single-universe account, and these are the issues discussed in this chapter.

The first section of the chapter outlines several of the difficulties that the theist will have to face and account for in accepting a multiverse theory. Some of these difficulties will not apply exclusively to theists; rather, they will apply to anyone considering the acceptance of a multiverse. With that in mind, however, each problem discussed in this section will be one that has to be faced by the theistic-minded multiverse proponent, nonetheless. The next section details how the theistic acceptance of a multiverse theory that calls for the existence of all possible universes entails a deistic God rather than the God of classical theism. And finally, in the last section, I discuss how various accounts of free will and determinism play out in the multiverse in light of a deistic God, showing how various conceptions and combinations of free will and determinism are compatible with the deistic multiverse theory for which I ultimately argue.

Before beginning, I think it is necessary to define precisely what I mean when I refer to theists or the theistic God. As I want this definition to be as inclusive as possible, it will be quite broad yet still set us up with a conception that is narrow enough to understand, grasp and implement. I will first begin with an outline of the God of which I will be discussing, and then from that, one can take a theist simply as one who believes in the existence of such a God. The kind of God of which I am speaking is the traditional "3-O" God of Judeo-Christian theism, attributing omniscience, omnipotence, and omnibenevolence (among other things) to Him. The three "omni" attributes are the most important for our concerns here, so the discussion of God will generally only be taken to be a conception in which these three attributes are essential. Of course, the interpretations of what exactly each of these particular divine attributes entails can be widely divergent but, for our purposes at the moment, the particularities and details of the attributes themselves can be set aside, rather the primary consideration is that God possesses these attributes, regardless of their particular interpretation. To be considered a theist one does not need to practice any active worship of this God, be of a particular denomination or organized religion, or anything of that sort, or even accept the veridicality of any particular scripture. The simple act of belief is enough to qualify some individual as a theist, in this sense. Being a theist is simply an ontological status or view, one that is distinct from any religious practice. While it may seem a bit out of place to discuss the attributes of and belief in the God of classical theism here, given that the overall project being presented makes a case for a deistic God, I feel that such a brief mention is necessary. The adoption of the God of classical theism, at this point, begins with establishing a set of attributes that He is traditionally thought to possess. This is done so that, following the discussion of the attributes of the deistic God that will come to be presented, the reader can reflect and see that the differences between the two interpretations of God (at least in terms of the attributes that they are said to possess) are minimal. The attributes of the deistic God that I will ultimately come to argue for do not vary at all from any of the attributes of the God of classical theism, rather they will simply require that we envision some of them in particular ways, and this will hopefully illustrate that if one is inclined to believe in the God of classical theism then he can perhaps be persuaded to believe in a deistic God without much amendment to his current beliefs, as the two are not quite as different as some may consider them to be.

THEISTIC CONCESSIONS IN ACCEPTING A MULTIVERSE THEORY

With all of the different types of multiverse models that have been discussed, there are some potential drawbacks for the theist if he accepts any of them. Of course, the degree to which the drawbacks will affect the theist will vary depending on the particular multiverse theory of which he is a proponent and on the particular ways in which he interprets the 3-O divine attributes, but they will exist, nonetheless. In the first case, some multiverse theories will entail the actualization of a whole host of universes that theists would not necessarily want to acknowledge as existing given the nature of their omnibenevolent God, so this is something for which the theist will have to account and explain. In the second case, multiverse theories will often take away from or discount the design argument, which is generally an argument put forth by theists to argue for the existence of God based on the unlikeliness that this universe could have arisen purely out of chance.[1] This argument, however, is generally most persuasive when applied to a single-universe ontological view, and would seemingly not work for the theist who is a proponent of multiverse theory. And in the final case, for multiverse theories that call for the actualization of all possible states of affairs,[2,3] there is an ethical issue with which the theist must deal. Multiverse theories that call for the actualization of all possible states of affairs raise interesting ethical problems since it seems an agent can remain indifferent to whether he ought to perform a good moral action or a bad moral action since whatever he does not do will be actualized in some other universe. This final difficulty is not exclusive to theists, as it will equally apply to all those who adopt a multiverse theory of this model; it is a difficulty that the multiverse theist will still have to face.

A substantial number of multiverse theories, especially those coming from the scientific perspective, argue for a multiverse that contains or exhausts every metaphysically possible universe. That is, they argue for a multiverse that contains or exhausts every universe that is physically possible given some range of set physical constants. If we are to limit our discussion to scientific multiverse models, then it seems that all of them entail the actualization of all possible universes, be their actualization and existence simultaneous to one another, be they part of an infinite series of big bangs and big crunches, wavepacket collapses, or of part of some other cyclical model.[4] Included within these actualized universes, then, would be a whole series of universes that either contain no sentient life, no life at all, significant amounts of evil and suffering, or are just on-balance "bad"[5] universes. The existence of many of these universes is potentially at odds with the conception of an omnibenevolent God that many theists hold, given that many theists would argue that God would create only universes that meet specific criteria. Surely there is nothing overtly illogical or incoherent about the existence of such "bad" universes, and there is no clear contradiction between them and the existence of God, but it remains that some theists may not want to concede the existence of, say, multiple universes containing an immense amount of pain and suffering, or universes in which there is no sentient life whatsoever. Furthermore, theists may not even want to concede that the existence of such universes is possible, and this is where the tension lies. While there is no explicit contradiction between the existence of God and the existence of all logically and metaphysically possible universes within a multiverse a contradiction could arise given certain specific interpretations of God's attributes and His nature.

The scientific multiverse accounts presented are generally concerned not with the content of the universes; rather, they are concerned purely with the physical constants and ways by which these universes can come into existence given quantum mechanics and laws of nature. The concern of physicists and mathematicians is not with the moral content of these universes— whether they are good or bad in relation to some arbitrary scale of worthiness; rather, they are merely concerned with the sheer existence of the universes. The theist, on the other hand, may place considerable importance on the content of the universe, concerned with things such as ethical considerations, overall goodness, inherent value, and the like. Because of this, the scientific approach to the multiverse in most, if not all, cases entails the existence of far more universes than does the theistic one. The theist who aims to adopt a multiverse view and to incorporate the scientific case for that multiverse will then be forced to reconcile this difference, which may be seen as a drawback for theists in accepting multiverse theories. Essentially, a concession concerning the scope of universe inclusion within the multiverse will need to be made, either on the theological side or on the scientific side. Proponents of the theistic multiverse may try to reconcile this difference by inserting a threshold, such that any universe that falls below this threshold given whatever value and method of measurement is being used is not even a possible universe and thus would not be actualized at any point within the multiverse. This approach, however, demands that the theist justify his threshold, both in where he chooses to place the threshold and in what it purports to value. He must also provide reasoning as to why this particular threshold is more suitable than other potential thresholds that are placed at other locations and value other variables. This will not entirely solve the problem for the theist though, since the scientific models would call for very different thresholds and would set out very different definitions of possible, so still the issue remains for the theist that scientific multiverse models entail the existence of far more universes than they would generally like to acknowledge as possible. So many universes that the theist may not want to accept as possible that it may even prove to be damaging to the theist's particular conception of God and how He operates.

The second potential drawback for the theist is that the multiverse theory undermines the design argument. Design arguments typically argue, in one way or another, that the universe appears to have been intelligently designed, which entails an intelligent designer, and that this intelligent designer is God (Ratzsch, 2010). The arguments generally "involve reasoning from seemingly purposeful features of the observable world to the existence of at least one supernatural designer" (Manson, 2003, p. 1). One particular example of such an observation and inference may be that the physical constants required to produce and sustain life are very narrow, and based on the fact that we see life in this universe, one can argue that it could not possibly be the case that all of these things simply came together by chance, but that the creation of something as complex as our universe would have required significant design and intent.[6] It is important to note that many design arguments do not explicitly posit the existence of God, rather they point to the existence of just some supernatural designer, and that a further step is needed to identify that supernatural creator as God (Manson, 2003, p. 1).[7] Design arguments, however, are typically used, and generally work better with, single-universe models rather than multiverse models. This is because such arguments appeal to the uniqueness of our particular universe, arguing that the chance of such a universe coming to exist as it has is virtually impossible without some sort of intent and creator behind it. Many multiverse theories, however, claim that since all possible universes have or will be actualized at some particular place or time, then the existence of a universe such as ours is not only highly likely but inevitable. For example, for proponents of cyclical multiverse models, it would merely be a matter of time before, at some point in the infinite sequence of universes coming into and going out of existence, our particular universe with all of these life-supporting features should come to exist.[8] So, while the multiverse is not a direct challenge to the theistic view, it does undermine one of the stronger arguments that theists often appeal to in making a case for the existence of God. On most multiverse accounts there is no need to posit the existence of God to account for the apparent design of our universe since the existence of a universe just like ours is inevitable and is simply one of the wide variety of possible universes that has been actualized or that will, at some point, be actualized.

Finally, in the case of the ethical problem that the theistic proponent of multiverse models that entail the actualization of all possible states of affairs it faces, the theist will have to explain just how a traditional conception of morality can be maintained or if it needs to be maintained at all, in such a multiverse model. The issue is that, for an agent, his motivation for doing morally good acts may become diminished, trivialized, or altogether lost since, whether he does the morally good act or not, it will be actualized in some universe within the multiverse by either himself or one of his counterparts. Robert Adams captures the sentiment of this problem in writing that any particular agent in any particular universe could reasonably ask himself "[w]hat is wrong with actualizing evils, since they will occur in some other possible [universe] anyways if they don't occur in this one" (1979, p. 195). Likewise, an agent's refusal to commit some morally evil act will only make it so that that evil does not occur in his particular universe, which will further entail that that same evil that he refused to actualize will be actualized by one of his counterparts in some other part of the multiverse. The possible conclusion that stems from this is that it appears to trivialize all of our ethical considerations since whatever we do, or don't do, will entail the opposite outcome in some other universe. On this, the motivation to perform morally good actions is seemingly lost since the agent could adopt an "if I don't do it another version of me will" sort of attitude, as is discussed by Adams (1979). David Lewis, however, replies to such a worry as directed at modal realism, but what he says about modal realism can be applied to our case of the multiverse as well. He argues that

> For those of us who think of morality in terms of virtue and honour, desert and respect and esteem, loyalties and affections and solidarity, the other-worldly evils should not seem even momentarily relevant to morality. Of course, our moral aims are egocentric. And likewise, all the more for those who think of morality in terms of rules, rights and duties; or as obedience to the will of God. (Lewis, 1986, p. 127)

Of course, such a reply is not readily accepted by everyone, and Yujin Nagasawa argues that the kind of reply provided by Lewis does not adequately solve the problem. Of such a reply, Nagasawa writes

> However, if the multiverse model in question is correct, it is difficult not to extend our concerns to other possible universes in our context because even if people in other possible universes are morally irrelevant to what we do in our universe they nevertheless exist and form part of God as the totality. (Nagasawa, 2015, p. 188)[9]

While ethical and moral issues of the kind faced by modal realists will have to be addressed by any multiverse theory, this is something that the theistic multiverse proponent will be harder-pressed to provide a response to and discuss how his model will deal with certain ethical considerations. A theistic multiverse account has the added layer and factor of God, and how ethics and morality relate to Him, to navigate whereas nontheistic multiverse accounts do not have this hurdle to deal with and thus can potentially avail themselves of many more possible responses.

THE MULTIVERSE ENTAILMENT OF DEISM

Now that several of the potential drawbacks that theists may face in accepting particular multiverse theories have been discussed, the attention now turns to how and why I think that the adoption of a specific kind of multiverse theory may entail deism if the proponent of the multiverse theory aims to maintain the existence of God. For purposes of clarity, I would like to specify the kind of multiverse model that I will be referring to, moving forward. It appears that most, if not all, of the strongest multiverse theories put forth by both science and philosophy entail the existence of all possible universes. There are two distinctions that differentiate each of these theories from one another, however. The first distinction is that each theory proposes its conception of how these universes exist in relation to one another. That is to say, these theories will vary in their explanations of the degree to which the universes within the multiverse are spatiotemporally distinct and isolated from each other, how and when the universes come to exist, how these multiple realities come to be actualized, and other similar factors. The second way in which these multiverse theories vary is in their conceptions of what exactly constitutes "possible" when referring to a possible universe. Some conceptions may argue that only universes that contain sentient life are possible, some may argue that only universes that possess a certain amount of goodness or happiness are possible, some may argue that any conceivable and logically possible universe is possible, while still others may argue that only universes that adhere with particular physical constants are possible. The variations among what ought to confer possibility upon a universe are wide and divergent, and this remains one of the most debated aspects of the multiverse discussion. When referring to the multiverse for the remainder of this project, unless otherwise indicated, the type of multiverse that is being referred to is this general kind that includes and exhausts all possible universes. That is to say, multiverses that entail the actualization, by whatever means and processes, of every possible universe, be it simultaneously, cyclically, part of an infinite sequence or any other mode. The key is that the multiverse models to which I refer when using the term "multiverse" are those that include, in some capacity, the actualization of all metaphysically possible universes. The individual conception of the relations of the universes to one another, as well as the conception of what exactly constitutes a possible universe, are not of extreme importance in this case since all types of these multiverse theories ultimately entail the same preference of a deistic God over the God of classical Judeo-Christian monotheism. So, while in this discussion, I will be speaking of an "all possible realities exist" kind of multiverse that is akin to modal realism (Lewis, 1986). This is done simply for the purposes of inclusion. What this means is that if my arguments seem plausible on this most extreme account of the multiverse, then surely it will plausibly transfer onto other brands of multiverse that happen to fall within this highly inclusive multiverse model. What I mean by "fall within" is that on the account that I am employing, very little (if any) restrictions are placed on what entails a possible universe, so any multiverse model that does propose any sort of definition that excludes some universes as impossible would be a multiverse that necessarily contains a numerically smaller amount of universes than does my inclusive model.[10] Any of those restrictions would then have to be argued for on their own basis, independently of my deistic argument. For example, suppose that the inclusive multiverse model contains 10,000 individual universes within it, and through all of these universes, every possible universe has been actualized. Now, if we take another multiverse model, let us call it *Multiverse C*, that includes a threshold claiming that only those universes that include sentient beings are truly possible, and thus are the only ones that can be included in the multiverse. Given this threshold, Multiverse C may contain only 5,000 individual universes.[11] Similarly, we can imagine another multiverse model, Multiverse D, that accepts as possible only those universes that contain sentient beings and that are also on-balance good, this model would contain only, perhaps, 3,000 individual universes. So, if my proposed arguments work on the level of the inclusive multiverse, since I make no claims as to whether a threshold for conference of existence really exists or, if it does exist, where it should be, any other multiverse models, such as those exemplified by Multiverse C or Multiverse D, would simply yield less individual universes for my proposal to range over. This is not a problem at all. The difference between multiverse models, for the scope of this project, is only that each one will include a different number of individual universes within it, and I have simply chosen the model that entails the largest number of individual universes within it to allow for my argument to range as broadly as possible.

The adoption of such a multiverse theory, for anyone who desires to maintain the existence of God, appears to be an ontological view in which this God would not be required to, or even feel compelled to, act in the natural world in any way aside from the initial act of creation. The reason for which an active God would be superfluous on a view such as this is that, given the fact that every possible universe is/was/will be actualized either at some particular time or at some particular space, this would entail that every possible state of affairs is/was/will be actualized as well. Given this, everything possible will happen in some universe at some time or in some place, so God's action would seemingly be pointless and unnecessary since He would simply be forcing the actualization of some particular state of affairs in one universe at one particular time over another at another particular time. It could not be the case that God loves one universe more than another and that this would cause Him to carry out some act on some particular universe (though we may want to think that we are the most important, this universe is merely indexical). Since God is all-loving, and His love is inexhaustible, there is no reason to think that God loves any one universe more than any other, and it is perhaps even an incoherent notion to suggest its possibility. Of course, whether it is even possible to think of God being infinitely loving yet still loving one thing more than another is a whole discussion in itself, but one that would require substantial thought and is not of immediate concern for our purposes here. But the simple position here is that God loves all of His creations equally and maximally, so while it may be nice to think that He loves us more than others, this is not the case. To suppose that God loves us more than other universes, or that He has a higher degree of concern for us than He does for other universes, and that He ought to actualize certain good states of affairs in our universe over others is simply an indexico-centric mindset, for lack of a better term.

While we cannot truly claim to know or understand what would motivate God to act in the natural world, I think that we can safely make the modest claim that if God is to act in the natural world it is to bring about some state of affairs that would not otherwise come to be were He not to act. It would be to actualize some good (ideally) that otherwise would not be realized, to prevent some evil that would not have otherwise been prevented, or to actualize some other state of affairs that is in line with His desires. This seems a perfectly normal thing to desire, or perhaps even expect of God, but these kinds of expectations and desires are not only ones that work best in a single-universe model; rather, they are expectations and desires that are only even coherent in a single-universe model.

As has been discussed, the multiverse model that we are using here is one that includes enough universes so that each possible state of affairs is actualized across the multiverse at some particular spatial location or at some particular point in time. No claims have yet been made concerning exactly what constitutes "possible," but that is not of tremendous importance yet. For the purposes of this discussion I like to assume the most inclusive, plausible form of what "possible" entails, generally referring to the idea of logically possible, but other multiverse models that employ a different ideal of possibility (as many theistic models would and do) are generally compatible with what I go on to argue. Furthermore, because this is a theistic multiverse model that we are working with, it will be assumed that God is the creator of each and every universe contained within the multiverse, as well as the creator of the multiverse itself. He is responsible for all that exists.

Now, given the nature of the multiverse that we are working with as well as the modest definition of what exactly it means for God to intervene in the natural world we can also think of what exactly it means for God to be perfectly good or omnibenevolent in our case. While in some cases the deistic God may be seen as being quite basic and as being a God of whom we can make no claims, aside from claiming that He created all that exists, that is not the case in this account. I do not employ a deistic conception of God that is essentially basic; rather, the deistic God that I propose is much closer to the God of classical theism than to the essentially basic notion. I will go into significantly more detail regarding the conception and attributes of the God that I propose in chapter 4, but for now all we need to focus on is the very basic sense in which I attribute perfect-goodness and omnibenevolence to Him. Again, a modest definition, one that I think is generally acceptable to most theists will be used. Here, when speaking of God, omnibenevolent or perfectly good and all-loving simply entail that He desires to maximize goodness and His love for and across all of His creations. This does not suggest that He act in any particular way or that He do particular things, since there will be many different interpretations of just what exactly goodness and love mean and just exactly how that goodness and love are to be achieved or demonstrated, but whatever those interpretations may be it still remains that God is fundamentally aimed at maximizing that goodness and maintaining that love. What this entails, for our purposes, is that God loves, equally and maximally, each and every universe within the multiverse (as well as the multiverse as a whole) and that He is fundamentally aimed at creating and maintaining the maximal amount of goodness possible within each universe in the multiverse.

If it is the case that the multiverse is composed of universes that collectively exhaust all possible states of affairs, that God's actions are done with the purpose of actualizing some possible state of affairs that otherwise would not have occurred, and that God's all-loving nature entails that He loves each of His universes equally and maximally, then this poses several problems for the theist if he hopes of maintaining a conception of God that includes any sort of intervention in the natural world. In either case, it seems that God's intervention in the natural world does not quite fit into the multiverse theory, either because it is simply not warranted or because it would be counter to a particular aspect of God's nature.

In the first case, God's decision to actualize one state of affairs in a particular universe would be superfluous since that state of affairs is/was/will be realized in another universe within the multiverse without His intervention. That is to say, there would seem to be no reason for God to intervene in the natural order of a particular universe in order to actualize some particular event that would already be actualized in some other universe somewhere else or at some other time without His intervention. For God, each and every possible event will come to pass naturally without His intervention, and if He desires to see such an event pass, then all He needs to do is locate, either spatially or temporally, the universe in which it will come to pass. While this may seem counterintuitive to say, God ought to, essentially, be indifferent to when and where this state of affairs will come to pass, so long as it comes to pass. We, on the other hand, will not be indifferent to when or where a particular event shall come to pass since we are confined to our particular universe and only have limited extension in time, but this is merely indexical, and factors that cannot and will not guide God's actions in any way. Setting aside competing views regarding God's conception of time and space, it simply does not appear that God would be moved to need to see some particular state of affairs actualized *right here* or *right now*, since these two concepts (on most accounts, I think) apply only to us, and not to God. For example, let us suppose that a freely acting agent, let us call her Gillian, is in a tricky situation in universe U^1. Gillian is trapped beneath a large boulder with nobody around to help her. She is trapped in such a way, and the boulder is so large that she will not be able to free herself by her own strength or determination. If Gillian is somehow able to be freed from beneath the boulder, she will go on to recover from whatever injuries she has sustained and continue to lead a normal and productive life, however, if she is not able to be freed from underneath the boulder then she will die within a very short period of time.

Without delving too much into the details of what kinds of actions God is able to perform (this will be given more consideration shortly), there does not appear to be anything precluding God from intervening to save Gillian from her untimely suffering and death. That is to say, there is no inherent logical impossibility in God exercising His omnipotence and simply having the boulder lifted up and off of Gillian, allowing her to move forward and live the rest of her life. For God though, having created a multiverse in which every possible state of affairs is actualized in some universe at some time and place, there simply would not seem to be any motivation for Him to intervene to save Gillian, since somewhere in the multiverse there would be another universe in which all of the states of affairs leading up to this moment are exactly the same, except where Gillian's counterpart is somehow freed from underneath the boulder by natural methods not requiring any divine intervention. Furthermore, there are actually a great many universes in which Gillian's counterparts are freed from underneath the boulder by natural means since there are a wide variety of states of affairs in which she is freed that are possible. For example, there is a universe, U^2, where the boulder simply rolls off of her, there is a universe, U^3, where a friend comes by and helps to remove the boulder, there is a universe, U^4, where the boulder crumbles apart and allows Gillian to remove herself, and so forth. In each of these universes, Gillian's counterpart is able to carry on with her life. For God to intervene in U^1 to save Gillian makes no difference in the scheme of the overall multiverse, for there is already a multitude of other universes in which Gillian counterparts are saved. Furthermore, again, since all possible states of affairs are actualized across the multiverse, God's intervention to save Gillian in U^1 would not yield any more good than simply allowing the natural course of events to play out since it would simply shift the burden of Gillian's death by boulder onto some other universe. That is to say, if Gillian does not die because of this boulder in U^1, then it will simply be her counterpart in U^2, U^3, or U^{45}, or any other universe who will. While the occurrence of whether or not this happens in a particular universe may be important to us, since we happen to live in a particular universe, it makes no difference to God, who is a resident of no particular universe. Because it makes no difference to God in which particular universe certain states of affairs come to pass, there lacks any motivation for Him to intervene in order to actualize any state of affairs in any particular universe at any particular time. There simply is no need to invoke God's intervention in order to actualize events that will already come to pass naturally.

In the second case, similar to the first, it seems that even if God were to act in a universe to actualize some particular state of affairs that otherwise would not have occurred there is still an immensely large number of other universes in which that possible state of affairs also would not have occurred, so God's decision to act in any one particular universe would seem arbitrary. Continuing on with our previous example of Gillian being trapped under a boulder, there are an extremely large number of universes in which Gillian (or one of her counterparts) is trapped under a boulder, so it would seem arbitrary if God were to intervene in only one universe, or to intervene in even in a small number of universes while leaving the other Gillian's to be crushed to death. The decision for God of which universe(s) to intervene in would have to be arbitrary. Arbitrarily making decisions and acting on them seems to be something inconsistent with God's nature since, given His omniscience, He would have to know of any possible factors that would cause Him to act in a favorable manner toward one universe over another.

Perhaps God's particular love of us, in our universe, would cause Him to act in certain ways, to remove certain evil states of affairs that persist for us, for example, some may argue. If, as discussed above, however, God has equal and maximal love for all of His universes, then that love cannot be a motivating factor. If God has an equal amount of love for each and every universe, then there is no difference between our universe and any of the other universes, if we are to evaluate them in such a way. Given this inability to differentiate between universes, God would then be left with two options. He can either (1) arbitrarily decide which universe to perform a particular intervention within, or (2) refrain from intervening in any universes at all.

When speaking of God, one would be hard-pressed to find any theist who would claim that God ever makes any sort of arbitrary decisions, with the theist often pointing toward God's omniscience as an explanation.[12] For if there are any factors that would motivate God to act in a particular way, God would know about them and appeal to them. In the case of divine intervention within an individual universe in the multiverse; however, God does not know of any motivating factors because there are simply none that exist to know about. While there may be motivating factors for us from our perspective, such as our desire to minimize suffering, to maximize happiness and pleasure, these motivations that would seemingly call on God to act in our universe are merely indexical. There is potentially an infinite number of others and personal counterparts contained in a potentially infinite number of other universes who are all wanting of the same things and subject to the same indexical motivating factors that result in an expectation or desire for God to intervene. For God, there is no notion of indexicality that applies to him with matters such as these, so He faces no issues relating to preference that would persuade Him to act in one way or another (at least none in the sense that we are talking about here). Given that there are no motivating factors present for God since all motivating factors would be equal across all universes within the multiverse, God's decision to intervene would then have to be arbitrary, which is something contrary to His nature. We cannot say that God would act in an arbitrary manner, making decisions and acting in ways for no reason at all. In cases where no reason guides Him, it simply seems much more likely to suspect that God would refrain from acting altogether.

Such a claim regarding motivated action does not apply solely to God; rather, it is a simple claim that we can see evidenced in our everyday life. Humans, animals, anything capable of action, will act only out of motivation. Of course, what counts as motivating factors and how certain beings will react to them will vary, but the principle remains. If I am not motivated by fear to scream out of fear then I will not scream out of fear, if a dog is not motivated to sleep by fatigue then he will not sleep, if a rock is not motivated to fall by gravity, then it will not fall. Similarly, if God is not motivated by anything to act in the natural world, then He will not act in the natural world, and it is simply not clear that any motivations that would move God to act in the natural world have been identified, given the multiverse model. The only plausible motivation left would be the desire to intervene purely for the sake of intervention, but this, again, does not seem in line with the overall nature of God.

SOME CONSIDERATIONS OF FREE WILL AND DETERMINISM IN THE DEISTIC MULTIVERSE

One issue surrounding the discussion of any kind of deistic multiverse thought concerns how exactly one is to interpret deism in relation to determinism and free will. This is a very important point of discussion for the simple fact that it may not be entirely clear how free will and determinism factor into deism. Deism itself is compatible with both free will and determinism, but while deism is certainly compatible with deterministic viewpoints it certainly does not entail determinism and, similarly, while deism is compatible with libertarianism it certainly does not entail it either. The same can be said of multiverse accounts. Specific deistic viewpoints will surely vary in their treatments of the free will and determinism debate but, generally speaking, there is no inherent entailment or preclusion either way. The deistic multiverse view that I forward is compatible with a range of points along the libertarian to determined continuum of how the multiverse, and its inhabitants, operate. The discussion below touches on four different possibilities of how the multiverse operates. If we are to imagine that we are speaking of free will and determinism appearing on a continuum, with the ability to display ultimate freedom being the extreme at one end of the continuum and ultimate determinism being the extreme at the other end of the continuum then we can imagine that any account of how freedom operates in the world would fall somewhere on or between these two points. Below I outline several different possibilities of how a deistic multiverse can be composed, with regard to free or determined universes, and discuss how they are compatible with the deistic multiverse that I forward. Of course, each of these different accounts of free will and determinism will come with its own share of problems and objections, particularly when being discussed in conjunction with divine attributes, but to engage in a full-fledged discussion of the nature of free will and determinism or of any of these difficulties is beyond the scope of this section and of the overall project. The aim of this section is simply to show that multiverse deism is compatible with a wide range of views related to free will and determinism, and to show how such views may play out in a deistic multiverse.

The first scenario is one that I refer to as the libertarian scenario and is one in which the multiverse allows for the total exercise of free will for those creatures who possess it. In this sense, God created the multiverse and each universe within it, while at the same time allowing for the creation of creatures who display the ability to have and exercise free will. Such a multiverse, if we are to return to looking at a free will and determinism continuum, would appear close to or exemplify the "ultimate free will" point of the continuum, with God having put in place no deterministic processes anywhere in the multiverse that would impede the freedom of the creatures possessing free will.

While it is possible that not all creatures in the multiverse to possess free will, our concern here is purely for the creatures that do. In creating the universe, while God may have had and continues to have certain desires about the way things should be, He holds the value of free will to be greater than His desires, in a sense. For example, while God may desire to see a multiverse that contains no moral evil, He places a higher value on the possession and exercise of free will than He does in His own desire not to see any moral evil. In this sense, it is simply one of God's desires taking precedence over another of His desires—namely, the desire to see His creations to display free will takes precedence over His desire to see a multiverse that contains no moral evil.

How such a conception is compatible with a deistic God seems quite evident, in that God would have gone about creating the universe in such a way as to allow for those creatures that He endowed with the capacities for free will and the ability to exercise that free will without any subsequent involvement from Him. Such a multiverse would, essentially, call for an inactive God based on the high value that has been placed on the possession and exercise of free will (presumably by God), regardless of any negative consequences that may happen to arise from that privilege.

The main drawback of such an ontological view is that it may pose problems and require varied interpretations of some of the divine attributes, namely omniscience. The proponent of this kind of operation of the world will have to present an account of just how, or whether, it is possible that divine omniscience can coexist simultaneously with true free will. The proponent will then have to provide further accounts of what kinds of limitations God's omniscience may have, and whether or not that has any bearing on any of the other divine attributes or the overall conception of God. Furthermore, the proponent of this view will also have to explain how, despite the appearance of the ability to make free choices in some aspects of life, we seem to face a great number of impediments (natural and otherwise) when it comes to exercising our will in many other aspects of life. For example, I may have the desire to fly, to walk on the moon or to memorize a long numerical sequence, but for reasons that seem to be beyond my control my ability to realize my will is beyond my abilities, and is impeded in quite an obvious way. So one who aims to support this libertarian viewpoint must provide an account of how these various impediments that seem to limit my freedom do not, in fact, pose a problem for him. Accomplishing such a task is no easy thing, so it is not clear to me that such an account of free will is even entirely plausible. That said, however, if it is the case that a proponent of this kind of account is able to provide adequate accounts that allow for him to satisfactorily reply to some of the potential drawbacks mentioned above then the account will still be compatible with a deistic multiverse.

Despite the fact that we do not appear to enjoy complete freedom in this universe, it is possible that this libertarian account is still actualized. So while the proponent of this kind of complete libertarian freedom may not be able to appeal to our universe for concrete examples to support his view, that does not entail that it is entirely implausible or nonexistent, it simply means that it may not be plausible or existent at this particular time in this particular universe.

The second scenario is one that I refer to as hard determinism. In this second scenario, God created the multiverse with a specific plan in mind of how He wanted each and every event to take place, both for natural processes and processes involving humans and other sentient beings.[13] This account does not allow for any kind of free will, so any free will that any of God's creations think that they have or seem to display is merely an illusion. All of the decisions that these creatures think that they freely make are not actually free, rather they are determined by God. This account is more compatible with the straightforward and traditional account of some of God's divine attributes, particularly omniscience. On this account, unlike other accounts that allow for free will, God has complete knowledge of each and every event, past, present, and future, and there does not seem to be a need to provide any further explanation on any limitations of God's knowledge.[14]

Such an account of determinism can be, in one case, equated to the account presented by Peter van Inwagen in his paper "The Incompatibility of Free Will and Determinism" (1982). Van Inwagen argues for a kind of determinism in which each and every state of affairs that comes to pass is determined by the conjunction of both an antecedent state of affairs and the absolute nature of laws of physics. That is to say, the laws of physics determine the state of affairs at time T_1 given the conditions of a state of affairs at some time T that immediately precedes T_1. If we are to expand this concept of determinism across all of the states of affairs over time then given the state of affairs at the initial starting point of the multiverse (or some specific universe within the multiverse) the laws of physics will determine the progression of each of the subsequent states of affairs that will ever come to be. It has been argued that such a conception of the operation of the universe can come to pass in one of two ways. The first is the more commonly conceived idea, and alluded to above, in which God put laws of physics and nature in place to guide the processes of the universe. The way in which the relevant laws were set up guarantees a certain path and outcome given the initial starting points. The second proposed way in which a determined universe could arise suggests that, in creation, God imparted each and every particle with a kind of "self-sustenance" characteristic (Kvanvig & McCann, 1988, p. 14). This self-sustenance characteristic would allow for the extension and continuation of all particles to carry on in a particular way without the subsequent intervention of God. Of course, the nature of this self-sustenance characteristic could be such that it allows for free will and the existence of undetermined processes, but so too is it compatible with the determined existence of these particles.

A deterministic account such as this would exemplify, quite fittingly, the extreme determinist point on the free will—determinism continuum and seems to be one that is, at least on the surface, most easily compatible with a deistic viewpoint. Such a deterministic viewpoint is compatible with the deistic multiverse in that it would call for God not just to create the multiverse in the beginning, but to also determine all subsequent events that would ever take place within that multiverse. Following the creation and determination of the multiverse, God would simply have to refrain from intervening in the multiverse in any way. This should be no problem, however, since in the initial act of creation God already determined all events that will ever come to pass, presumably in a way that He would desire them to come to pass, so it is not clear that there would ever be a need for Him to intervene in any way. One could generally assume that such determined events would come to pass due to the presence of natural laws put in place by God at the time of creation, and Michael Ruse seems to call for such a conception in saying that "one might well argue that the designer [God] always works through laws" (Ruse, 2003, p. 319). That is, the physical laws put in place essentially act on behalf of God, ensuring His will is done, removing any need for His intervention in the natural world.

Potential drawbacks to views like this, however, come from arguments such as the problem of evil. Atheists could argue that, on this account, God would have had to have not only known about or allowed but determined all of the evil that takes place in the world, both natural and moral. This sort of claim would seriously bring into question whether or not He is a perfectly loving and omnibenevolent God, in that all evil that we see across the multiverse would be not just permitted (actualized, in a weak sense) by God but fully determined by God. The proponent of this kind of determined ontological view would have to find some way to account for a multiverse that appears to have a great deal of gratuitous evil in it as well as a God who has determined, and is seemingly directly responsible for, each and every event that takes place.

In the third scenario, one that I refer to as soft determinism, it is possible that God created a multiverse that is both determined and contains free will.[15] Without getting into an extended discussion about compatibilism and incompatibilism, I think that such an account of free will and determinism is plausible, and perhaps even more likely than some of the other alternatives discussed in this section. In a universe such as this, God has determined various outcomes and events in our lives, but He is rather unconcerned with how exactly we go about getting to those particular outcomes. One way to think about it is to say that God, on this account, will generally be more so concerned with the "big picture" events rather than the "small picture" events that happen between them. Surely, the division of what constitutes big versus small picture events will vary from account to account, but the core ideal here is that God is concerned only with, and determines only, certain selected states of affairs within the multiverse. For example, God may determine that I go on to be a great basketball player, but He does not determine how and by what methods I decide to practice basketball. Those decisions are left up to me and are my free choices. Similarly, God may determine that the human race will drive itself into extinction by some predetermined point in time while leaving it open how such an extinction will come to pass. The extinction can come via world pollution, exhaustion of food supplies, war, disease or some other method, but all of the decisions leading up to that point remain free for humans to exercise their free will. Another way to conceptualize such a view is to think of the general path of life, history, or time as a road with walls on either side. As we are travelling down this road we have the ability to veer left or to veer right, making our exact path toward each destination slightly varied due to our individual free choices, but we are only able to freely choose to veer so far in one direction before we are confronted with the walls that guide us in one particular way.

One way in which God may choose to facilitate such a multiverse is through the introduction of natural laws. Natural laws, essentially, act as God's walls on either side of the road, allowing us to make free choices within certain bounds and preventing us from using our freedom to stray too far in certain directions. Just as our free will may give us the desire to fly or to breathe underwater, the natural laws are set up in such a way as to prevent us from doing those things (and a variety of other things that we may desire to do).

Such an ontological view is compatible with a deistic account because there is no requirement for God to act in or on the multiverse at any time following creation. While God may determine certain events or states of affairs that continue to happen within the multiverse on a daily basis, all of these things would be facilitated either by the introduction of natural laws or through the endowment of the self-sustenance capacity at the time of creation. These natural laws and self-sustenance capacities, essentially, act as God's agent, ensuring that whatever states of affairs He wants to see come to pass and also allowing for free will to be exercised in those states of affairs about which God has no particularly strong desire. A system like this allows for God to determine certain states of affairs in the multiverse while allowing for the possession and exercise of free will without violating any of the core principles of deistic thought and without requiring any divine intervention within the multiverse.

The final scenario is one similar to soft determinism, but instead of just having some free events and some determined events coexist in the same universe, there are free universes and determined universes that coexist within the multiverse. As there is nothing inherent in multiverse deism that precludes an assortment of differently determined universes[16] it is possible that some universes within the multiverse may be entirely determined (hard determinism universes), some universes in the multiverse may be entirely free (libertarian/free will universes), and still some may contain both determined events and events brought about by acts of free will (soft determinism universes). While God may have wanted to have some universes completely determined, some universes completely free, and some universes containing both elements of freedom and determinism, God created a multiverse that is comprised of a multitude of universes, collectively exemplifying a great number of points along the free will—determinism continuum. While I previously argued for the apparent implausibility of extreme libertarian views of free will in our own universe, the overall view presented in this section is one in which such libertarian universes could exist elsewhere within the multiverse alongside other kinds of universes. Despite the apparent implausibility of such libertarian accounts, given the existence of the natural laws and physical constants that we see in our universe, there is nothing about multiverse deism (in a broad sense) that requires that all universes within the multiverse display similar natural laws or physical constants or even that all universes within the multiverse display any natural laws or physical constants at all.[17]

Since, as we have seen through the individualized discussions of each kind of universe above, there is no inherent incompatibility between any of these kinds of universes and a deistic ontological view, and it does not appear that there is any incompatibility between any of these kinds of universes coexisting within the same multiverse, then such a scenario ought surely to be compatible with, if not required by, a deistic multiverse view.

CONCLUSION

In this chapter we have defined, in a very general sense, that the kind of God we are working with is the God of Judeo-Christian tradition, exemplifying the three omni attributes of omniscience, omnipotence, and omnipotence. The precise interpretations of any or all of these three attributes are not of extreme importance when talking about God, at this point, rather the main point of emphasis is merely that He possesses them in some capacity. We have also discussed some of the potential difficulties that will have to be dealt with given the theistic acceptance of a multiverse theory that calls for the existence of all possible universes. Particularly, the disconnect between the types of universes called for to populate the multiverse on theism and those called for on scientific approaches, the problem of having to deal with the potential multiverse undermining of design arguments and, finally, the moral indifference that may arise from the existence of counterparts in a multiverse theory are all potential problems for proponents of the theistic multiverse.

Given the theistic acceptance of the multiverse, we have also discussed how the acceptance of the God of Judeo-Christian tradition along with the acceptance of a multiverse theory that calls for the existence of all possible universes entails the acceptance of a deistic God rather than the God of classical theism. This entailment arises as a result of two factors: (1) that any action by God in a multiverse that is comprised of all possible universes is superfluous and unnecessary, and (2) that any action taken by God in a multiverse that is comprised of all possible universes is arbitrary since He would be in possession of no motivating factors to cause Him to act, and for God to act arbitrarily and beyond any type of motivation is contrary to His nature.

Finally, some considerations with regard to the compatibility of different ontological views of free will and determinism with the deistic multiverse were discussed. It was demonstrated that the deistic multiverse, while it entails neither of them, is compatible with a libertarian view, a deterministic view, and compatibilist views, both on the scales of single universes and in the multiverse as a whole.

NOTES

1. Of course, this is a short generic description of a rich and diverse body of literature, but it serves no immediate purpose here to delve into the intricacies of individual specific versions of the design argument.

2. I assume that all multiverse theories of this type also call for the existence of individual counterparts.

3. The use of "all possible states of affairs" is intended to account for both all possible types of universes and all possible universe-histories within each of those possible types of universes.

4. See Deutsch (1997), Norris (1999), Linde (1987).

5. There are a variety of ways in which a universe can potentially be labeled as "bad" but the specifics of this are not of tremendous importance here.

6. This is more of an example of the fine-tuning argument from design, but there are other variations of the design argument, such as the cosmological and eutaxiological arguments (Manson, 2003, p. 2).

7. With that in mind, we will still assume that step—that if there is a supernatural designer, then it would be God, for our purposes.

8. White (2003) discusses various aspects and possibilities of this line of thought.

9. Here, Nagasawa is discussing the ethical issue in relation to multiverse pantheism, but it is still easy to see how such a response works in our context.

10. Just as the amount of possible universes in Tegmark's level 1 multiverse is less than the number of possible universes in his level 4 multiverse. The same idea is at play here.

11. The exact figure is not important. The only thing of importance to note is that the figure will be smaller than that of the one within the inclusive multiverse.

12. While not in the exact same context, Forrest (2012) argues that God is not able to act arbitrarily.

13. I use the term "natural process" to differentiate between processes of nature, such as waves coming and going, trees growing, and so forth, from any kind of processes that are seemingly initiated by the actions of any sentient beings.

14. Or at least significantly less explanation that account that require a limited sense of omniscience.

15. While I do not utilize the traditional definition of soft determinism, I think that the kind of theory that I am discussing shares enough similarities with the traditional definition to allow me to reasonably maintain use of this term.

16. In fact, there could be cases in which multiverse deism could *require* such an assortment, based on the exhaustion of all logical possibilities.

17. This can vary depending on the type of multiverse account being adopted. The multiverse account that I have adopted for our purposes here is that every logically possible universe exists, and there does not appear to be anything logically flawed in asserting that universes without natural laws or physical constants can exist within the multiverse.

Chapter 4

Attributes of a Deistic God

In the previous chapter, I argued that if a theist opts for a multiverse ontological view, then this view entails a deistic God. As such, I think it is only necessary that I now provide an account of just what exactly this deistic God is and what we can say about Him. That is to say before one can even begin to consider my argument as plausible, it must first be spelled out precisely what kind of God I envision and what kind of attributes He possesses. Hopefully, such a discussion will provide an enhanced level of clarity as to how the adoption of a particular kind of multiverse paired with a particular conception of God entails a deistic multiverse rather than a theistic one. This discussion will also help to paint a clearer picture of the kind of God that I ultimately argue for and the kinds of attributes that He possesses, given the designation of deistic. Through this chapter, I also hope to show how a deistic God and His attributes are not too different from the God of classical theism and His traditional attributes (as were discussed in chapter 3), allowing for the gap between classical theism and deism to be substantially narrowed.

The structure of this chapter will begin with a discussion on the overall vagueness of the nature of the deistic God, and some of the potential reasons behind that lack of clarity. Given such a lack of explicit divine attributes or interpretations of particular divine attributes within deism, which is discussed in this chapter, I take the overall conception of the deistic God to be somewhat open to interpretation. Because of this lack of clarity, moving through this chapter, I discuss my interpretations of omnipotence and omnibenevolence, respectively, as they relate to the deistic conception of God. The section entitled *Other Attributes: Omniscience, Timelessness, Immutability and Necessity* discusses, as one would expect, omniscience, timelessness, immutability, and necessity. For our purposes here, these are some of the divine attributes that do not seem to have as much of a bearing on the overall deistic conception as those discussed in the preceding two sections but still must be addressed in a discussion such as this. Finally, the last exploratory section in this chapter discusses how each of the particular interpretations of the divine attributes discussed to that point ultimately factor into the overall conception of the deistic God.

INTRODUCTION TO DEISM

In reviewing the literature, of various sorts, on deism, it is challenging to pin down a detailed account of just what exactly the nature of a deistic God is and what exactly deism entails.[1] The vagueness of the true nature of deism, and what an adequate definition of it would be, is articulated pointedly by S.G. Hefelbower in his 1920 essay where he writes that "[t]here is no accepted definition of Deism. If you try to find out what it is from the books and articles that discuss it you will be left in confusion" (Hefelbower, 1920, p. 217). Despite this acknowledged lack of clarity (or perhaps precisely *because* of it) Jonathan Kvanvig and Hugh McCann offer their take on what exactly deism entails by saying,

> On this view, God is conceived as a sort of cosmic engineer Who, in the beginning, created a world that operates according to certain immutable laws, including laws of conservation. Once the universe was in place, it was no longer necessary for God to be active in sustaining it, nor is it so today. He may, on some accounts, intervene periodically to cause certain adjustments or changes within the universe or its operations, but no continuous activity on God's part is needed simply to keep it in existence. Although deistic accounts of creation usually appeal to immutable laws as the explanatory device that allows for God's inactivity, it is worth noting that a more Aristotelian conception of nature leads to a very similar view. Instead of claiming that laws, conceived as relations between types of events, explain how God need not be active, one might claim that in creating, God implants a capacity for self-sustenance in what He creates, and that it is the presence or operation of this capacity that absolves God from sustaining the world after His initial creative activity ceases. Indeed, a theory that exempts God from directly sustaining the universe by appealing to laws must ultimately ground the truth of those laws in the characteristics of the things whose behavior the laws describe, and so must in the end appeal to a self-sustaining capacity of the things God creates. (Kvanvig & McCann, 1988, p. 14)

Even despite this description of the nature of deism (and the two distinct methods by which God could have enacted it), Kvanvig and McCann have still yet to detail any characteristics of the deistic God that distinguish Him from the God of classical theism aside from the deistic God being precluded from acting in the natural world. That is, while they have detailed what deism entails, nothing substantial is said about the nature of the deistic God Himself.

There are hundreds of books and papers devoted to the discussion of the attributes of the God of classical theism,[2] coming together to form an expansive body of literature on the topic, but the same simply cannot be said about attributes of the deistic God. Very little is written detailing the attributes of the deistic God or saying much about the intricacies of His nature. This could be because many of the deistic writers feared persecution by the church by being labeled as atheists so they did not want to explicitly put into writing their particular views on God, let alone go into substantial detail about the attributes of such a God out of fear of being labeled an atheist (Vailati, 1998, p. ix; Sullivan, 1982, p. 209).[3] On the other hand, perhaps very little is said of the nature of a deistic God for reasons of simplicity. That is to say, that a deistic God could possibly be essentially basic and aside from Him being the creator we cannot, with any certainty, ascribe Him any attributes because of our epistemic limitations. Essentially, "[i]f there is a God, he is infinitely beyond our comprehension, since, being indivisible and without limits, he bears no relation to us. We are therefore incapable of knowing either what he is or whether he is" (Krailsheimer, 1995, p. 122) but this is not the kind of God that I envision or call for.

Since generally emerging in the enlightenment period, in the mid-seventeenth century, the exact conception of deism has been used differently over the centuries, with it being used to describe "the opinions of men who believed in a religion that could be achieved by reason apart from Christian revelation" (Sullivan, 1982, p. 206), to Englishmen often identifying deism with Unitarianism from the late-seventeenth century through the eighteenth century (Sullivan, 1982, p. 206). Also, in the seventeenth century, as mentioned above, deists could be labeled or viewed as atheists because they were seen as "those who deny immaterial things" (Sullivan, 1982, p. 209) which would, in essence, make them indistinguishable from atheists, or it could otherwise be argued that "since the ranks of atheism included all who denied God's creation or government of the world, they included deists; those who adopted the less offensive title were attempting to disguise their real allegiance" (Sullivan, 1982, p. 209). Needless to say, many of the descriptions of deism carried with them negative connotations, which may be what points toward the general lack of desire to subscribe to deism or to engage in substantial discussion about it. To be fair, among these varying accounts of the entailment of deistic thought there were accounts that seem to capture the essence of the kind of deism that I have in mind when I speak about it, such as one that describes deism by saying that "[t]he normative construction entails an understanding of God's relation to the created order that denies that He is either present or immanent in the world and limits His role to the act of creation and the establishment of laws which have since ruled the universe" (Sullivan, 1982, p. 213). Similarly, William Bristow points out the common thread that seems to run through all of the accounts of deism when he describes it by saying,

> According to deism, we can know by the natural light of reason that the universe is created and governed by a supreme intelligence; however, although this supreme being has a plan for creation from the beginning, the being does not interfere with creation; the deist typically rejects miracles and reliance on special revelations as a source of religious doctrine and belief, in favor of the natural light of reason. (Bristow, 2010)[4]

While these latter two interpretations of deism seem to be much more in line with what I have in mind and also carry far less of a negative connotation as some of the other interpretations mentioned above, it must also be remembered that all of these interpretations were in play at, more or less, the same time across Western Europe, rendering the public discussion of deism a risky business. This is perhaps one of the reasons that there were very few public deists and even fewer of them who were bold enough to put their views regarding the true nature of the view and its entailments in writing. Because of this lack of clarity and specificity expressed by the historical deistic literature, both from the deists themselves and from their opponents, with the exception of being precluded from acting within the natural world after its initial creation, I have taken the conception of the deistic God to be quite open to interpretation. Through that, I see the deistic God being compatible with a wide variety of attributes and interpretations of those attributes.

Because of the openness of the nature of the deistic God it is not clear that any deistic account need adhere to any particular conception of God,[5] and so any deistic account is, therefore, open to detail its account of God in any way it so chooses, so long as it is in accordance with the core principles of deism.[6] This leaves open many different possibilities for the nature of God, ranging anywhere from a super-basic God who has no features that we can attribute to Him, to a God who is quite similar to the God of classical theism, about whom much has been said. The deistic God that I will propose is far closer to the latter than to the former, and this is for several main reasons.

The first reason that I opt for a conception of God that does not stray too far from the classical conception is for the sake of simplicity and understanding. I find it far easier to conceptualize, understand, and ultimately make the case for a God who possesses a set of anthropomorphic attributes, much the same as the God of classical Judeo-Christian monotheism. It is simply far more understandable to discuss a God who possesses a maximal level of many of the same attributes that we do than it is to try to understand a highly abstract

God about whom we cannot make any claims. There is simply no need to go about complicating the classical conception of God by making a variety of substantial amendments to how we should conceive of His attributes. The second reason, closely related to the first that I have opted to propose the kind of God that I do is because there is simply no need to unnecessarily import a variety of amendments and qualifications to the classical conception of God. My overall argument that a theistic multiverse entails deism works fine without much modification to the classical conception of God, so there is no need to go about complicating the matter by removing or replacing a variety of long-standing divine attributes. Furthermore, to call for the abandonment of many of these attributes would draw me deep into the middle of a philosophical debate that I do not necessarily want to be in, just quite yet. To be fair, my account of a deistic God requires that certain divine attributes be interpreted and conceptualized in specific ways, but this is something that is not particular to my account of God. Importantly, mine will not be interpretations and conceptualizations that are not already in play within discussions of theology or philosophy of religion today. And finally, the third reason for adopting a conception of God that is closer to the classical conception of God than not is that it allows for a view that is more likely to be accepted by current classical theists, as a transition from their belief system to the one that I propose will not require a wholesale abandonment of the God that they have come to believe in. It would, in my view, be pointless to put forth an ontological view that is very unlikely to be accepted or viewed as plausible by the people at whom it is directed, so if it is possible to make the view clearly distinct yet maintain a number of the core values of the original ontological view for which it is being proposed as an alternative then it bodes well for the general acceptance of that new ontological view.

This discussion of the divine attributes of my conception of a deistic God will concern itself primarily with providing accounts for omnipotence, omnibenevolence and, to a lesser degree, omniscience since these three are typically considered to be the three essential attributes of God. While I do not wish to discount the overall importance of other divine attributes of which we can discuss as part of the deistic God's nature, omnipotence and omnibenevolence are the two most important ones for our purposes, and thus will garner the majority of the discussion. As they are typically thought to be the contingent attributes of God (with the exception of omniscience), other attributes such as omniscience, timelessness, immutability, and necessity will factor into the overall conception of the deistic God, but only minimally at this stage, and it is not entirely clear that any major issues will arise as a result of holding a particular conception of either of those divine attributes (unlike with omnipotence and omnibenevolence) so for that reason, discussion of them will be quite brief.

OMNIPOTENCE

At quick glance, many could take God's omnipotence to entail that He can do absolutely any task possible—a sort of unlimited and infinite power over anything and everything. This kind of omnipotence, a kind that René Descartes argues for, is one that I think is too strong. Descartes argues it is wrong to say or think that God can only do those tasks that can be described in a logically coherent way (Frankfurt, 1964, p. 262). Included within these seemingly impossible tasks that God can perform are such things as drawing a square circle, making 2+2=7, and creating a stone so heavy that God Himself cannot lift it (Frankfurt, 1964, p. 262).[7] For God, argues Descartes, to carry out logically impossible tasks is the ultimate display of His power, and since God's power ought to be unlimited, there is no reason that logical possibilities ought to play any factor in determining His abilities. The kind of omnipotence that I want to attribute to a deistic God, however, is still one of the stronger kinds of omnipotence that we can attribute to Him, without going so far as to claim that logical impossibilities are meaningless for God's abilities. While it does not entail ultimate and unlimited power, the various tasks that God is unable to do are tasks that, for God, are not even accomplishable tasks in the first place. Not being accomplishable tasks, God's inability to carry them out poses no threat to being able to attribute omnipotence to Him (Mavrodes, 1963).

Of the debate surrounding the nature of God's omnipotence, Nick Trakakis says that "[n]o matter how much controversy and debate may currently surround the extraordinary attribute of divine omnipotence, there is virtually complete consensus amongst philosophers and theologians that Aquinas is correct in saying that 'anything that implies a contradiction does not fall under God's omnipotence'" (Trakakis, 1997, p. 55) so, for that reason, I do not choose to move forward with a Cartesian view of omnipotence. The view of omnipotence that I am adopting is very similar to, if not the same as, the view forwarded by George Mavrodes (1963) and does not argue for the irrelevance of logic when it comes to God's abilities to carry out specific tasks. Mavrodes argues that God's abilities are limited by logic, in that He cannot carry out tasks that are logically impossible. In addition to that, due to God's nature, there are specific tasks that, while they may be logically possible to carry out for you or I, are not logically possible for God. The example used by Mavrodes is asking whether or not God can create a stone too heavy for Himself to lift, a classic dilemma traditionally used to question God's omnipotence. For if God cannot create a stone too heavy for Him to lift then, through His inability to create such a stone, there is clearly at least one task that He cannot carry out, whereas if He can create the stone too heavy for Him to lift, through His inability to lift the stone there is still clearly another task that He cannot carry out. So no matter how the question is answered, it seems that we arrive at the same conclusion: there is a task that is not inherently self-contradictory that God cannot perform, which means that God is not omnipotent. For Mavrodes, even though such a task contains nothing self-contradictory for you or I, for a being whom we already view as omnipotent, this is a self-contradictory task, and cannot be appropriately seen as an object of power. He calls tasks like this "pseudo-tasks" (Mavrodes, 1963, p. 223) and claims that the inability of God, or any omnipotent being, to carry out these pseudo-tasks is not damaging to the doctrine of omnipotence.

This account of omnipotence put forth by Mavrodes (1963), is of the type that I adopt for the account of the deistic God, but I must also expand on it, as it does not presently range far enough to be applied to the current discussion. Mavrodes's account does not discuss much of what kinds of tasks are to be considered pseudo-tasks, aside from the obvious ones such as drawing a square circle, or of creating a stone too heavy for God to lift. I will extend this list of pseudo-tasks to include tasks that are not within God's nature. That is to say, it cannot be considered an object of power to expect God to perform tasks that are not within His nature, and thus if He cannot perform tasks that are not within His nature, it ought not to be viewed as detrimental to the doctrine of omnipotence. This will be another case in which specific tasks, while they are possible to be carried out by us since there is no apparent contradiction precluding us from acting against our general nature, cannot be carried out by God since His nature is absolute to a maximal degree.

One example of something that would be out of God's nature would be to, as mentioned in chapter 3, act in an arbitrary manner (Forrest, 2012, p. 342). Given God's omniscience, it would seem that He would have all of the relevant information in any given situation, allowing Him to make a clear decision on whether or not to act in a particular manner. God's decision on whether to act or not would necessarily be guided by some sort of motivating factor.[8] Arbitrary decisions, however, by their very nature, seem not to be guided by any motivating factors whatsoever,[9] and can be seen as decisions made without knowing some particular piece of information that would grant motivation on some particular course of action.[10] That is to say, one who acts in an arbitrary manner is simply ignorant of the information that would allow him to make an informed decision that would motivate his action. In the absence of any motivating factors, we would expect that God would perform no actions whatsoever, given that He simply has no reason to act, and it is not at all clear that God would act simply for the sake of acting. So to expect God to perform any arbitrary actions is simply not possible since it is not within His nature. It is not within His nature to act without any motivation, and it is also perhaps meaningless to say that an action is arbitrary for God, since it would seem to deny Him some sort of information or specific knowledge that would allow Him to make a motivated decision, which is something that is not possible given His omniscience. So, for God to act in an arbitrary manner, while it may be possible for us, given God's omniscience and inability[11] to act unmotivated, such a task is not really a task and, on Mavrodes's terminology, would be reduced to a pseudo-task whose precluded actualization cannot damage the doctrine of omnipotence for God.

Another example of something that would be out of God's nature is to act in a less than perfectly efficient way. Given God's great power and knowledge, not only does He know the most efficient way to achieve certain ends but He also has the ability to do whatever is necessary in order to achieve those ends in the most efficient manner. For a being with such abilities, it would seem unnatural and unnecessary to go about actualizing some sort of desire by any way other than the most direct and efficient way. Given this, acting in a less than perfectly efficient way is something that we ought to include in the realm of actions that are not within God's power to do, but nonetheless poses no threat to His omnipotence. Let us apply this directly to the case of creation and divine intervention so as to provide a way to conceptualize this idea. In creating the world and all of the natural laws that govern it, God would have had the foresight and ability to create a world that carries on exactly how He so chose. That is to say; He could have set up the initial physical conditions of the world in such a way as to allow for the natural laws to guarantee that certain events come to pass exactly as He would have wanted them to. To assert that God needs to intervene in the natural world following its creation in order to actualize some state of events that He desires is simply to assert that God is acting in a less than perfectly efficient manner. To say that God intervenes in the natural world is to say the He is amending His initial creation, and for a being who could have created the world to play out in precisely the way that He wanted, the addition of divine intervention seems to be an unnecessary complication signaling something less than perfection.

Let us explore the concept of divine efficiency through an example that many of us will be familiar with. Let us imagine that Chris and Paul are both in the same upper-level philosophy course in their final year of university. They are both tasked with the final assignment of writing a philosophy paper on epistemic justification regarding miraculous events. Let us also imagine that there is some objective marker that denotes a perfect philosophy paper, something greater than merely a 100 percent grade, rather something transcendent that make it THE perfect paper. Now, let us finally imagine that upon the due date of the assignment, both Chris and Paul independently, yet simultaneously, turn in assignments that are both identical and exemplify the perfect philosophy paper. Now, given that two final products are identical, how exactly are we to determine which of these two young men displayed more power in producing their respective philosophy papers?[12] In order to make such a decision, given the identical nature of the products, we must explore the process by which each product came to be. In the first case, Chris wrote his philosophy paper in the traditional way with which many of us are familiar. Chris began by writing an outline for his paper, a draft, revised the draft by going through and making major and minor changes to his ideas, structure and overall presentation, and concluded with an editing stage in which he corrected all of the factual, grammatical and spelling errors that remained. After going through this process of construction, revision, and correction over a period of time, Chris ended up with the perfect philosophy paper which he promptly submitted. On the other hand, Paul simply sat down at his desk and wrote his paper from start to finish. He did not go back to make any revisions, he did no editing and simply ended up with the perfect philosophy paper which he, like Chris, promptly submitted. Now, if we are to choose which of these two young men displayed more power in writing identical perfect philosophy papers, I would argue that it was Paul because of the high degree of efficiency with which he carried out his task. Surely, to be able to write the perfect philosophy paper is a great display of power, by any standards, but to write one in the most efficient way possible, namely without having to go back and make any corrections or revisions, is a greater display of power. Given two identical outcomes, the most desirable, powerful, and best process of arriving at that outcome will generally be the most efficient one. Just as it is less efficient for us to write a philosophy paper using no punctuation and then go back and revise it by adding punctuation afterward than it is to write a perfect philosophy paper in the first place, it is less efficient for God to intervene in the world to actualize some particular state of events when He could have initially created the world in such a way that that state of affairs would come to pass naturally anyways. Now, rather than having just one thing govern the operation of the natural world (the natural laws), there is another entity that has been added to the equation to account for other aspects of the operation of the natural world (God). To be fair, it would be no extra effort for God to both create and introduce natural laws to govern the operation of the world while at the same time choosing to actively intervene within it, but this is simply an unnecessary and extra level of complication to the explanatory account of the processes in our world. So, just as Paul ought to be credited with the possession of greater power for his display of efficiency, so too must the deistic God.

Now, applied directly to our case of the multiverse, this would mean that, in creating the multiverse, God would be able to set it up in such a way as to allow for each and every event in the multiverse to occur exactly as He so chose (if there happened to be any events that He desired to occur at some particular time or at some particular place). To expect God to intervene in the natural order of things is to expect that He take an indirect route[13] in bringing about those particular desired events, where having taken a direct route (namely, initially setting it up so that the events would come to take place without His intervention) would have been more efficient and required no extra effort at all. There is simply no reason to think that God would take anything less than a direct route in actualizing His will and, as such, it would be against His nature to do so. Following the reasoning from above, performing such a task is not in the nature of God and, therefore, it is not really a task, rather it is a pseudo-task whose preclusion poses no threat to the doctrine of omnipotence. So, just as we cannot reasonably expect God to act in nature, and we can go so far as to preclude the possibility of Him acting in nature, we also cannot deem His inability to do so as detrimental to His omnipotence. Of course, the objection can be raised that the most efficient way for any process to be carried out is for God to simply intervene and actualize it Himself, rather than taking the indirect route of setting up natural laws that then govern the actualization of these processes. The problem with such an objection that calls for simplicity, however, is that there is no debate that natural laws are in place and are functioning to facilitate natural processes in our universe, and by positing an active God to explain the actualization of some processes a second mode of operation now becomes present in our universe. So, in calling for simplicity through the insertion of an active God, such an objection actually muddies the waters by adding a secondary mode of actualization to work alongside the evident laws of nature. To posit this additional mode of actualization is merely inefficient and unwarranted.

OMNIBENEVOLENCE

The sense in which I attribute omnibenevolence to God is a straightforward and general one. To say that God is omnibenevolent, on my account, is simply to say that He wants the best for His creations. Of course, such a definition is open to broad and divergent interpretation, and this is intentional. Again, one of the aims in spelling out the conception of the deistic God that I am working with is to provide an account of a God that is compatible with a wide variety of theistic views and interpretations, so it is for that reason that once I have captured, what I think is, the essential feature of omnibenevolence then any further qualifications regarding it are to be taken up in dialogue elsewhere, as these details are not of crucial importance to the current discussion. My account makes no claims with regard to what entails "best" for God's creations, or even what ought to compose the "creations" of which we ought to give consideration when considering wanting the best for them. All of these remain open to interpretation, and such interpretations will have to be argued for individually on their own accord. Here is not the place to carry out such a discussion as I do not see that any reasonable interpretation of either of these two terms will be incompatible with or yield any substantially undesirable conclusions for multiverse deism. With that in mind, however, in order to clarify and paint a more explanative picture of my general account of omnibenevolence, I will discuss how the addition of several different qualifications to my account will play out within the deistic multiverse. While some of these additional amendments will lead us to make, perhaps, some concessions that we do not really want to make, it will be important to remember that these further amendments are simply for the purpose of example and contextualization and that I am not making an argument for any of these additional qualifications; instead I am simply demonstrating how further specifications within my general account of omnibenevolence will play out in the deistic multiverse for those who happen to forward those particular views.

In the first case, we can look at various accounts of what the term "best" may entail in the idea that God wants the best for His creations. This can be interpreted in a number of ways. It is possible that some can see what is best for us as equating to what makes us the happiest, while others equate it to what is most just for us, or what provides us with the best overall health over the course of our lifetimes, or of how much freedom we enjoy. Whether best entails maximal happiness, justice, health, freedom, any other possible good, or some balanced combination of all of them, the same principle for omnibenevolence underlies all of them. Regardless of what the interpretation of "best" is, it is still the case that God wants the best for His creations. What each of these different interpretations will do, however, is alter the makeup of the multiverse. That is, a multiverse in which God wants the best for all of His creations, and best is to be interpreted as a maximal level of happiness may look entirely different from a multiverse in which God wants the best for all of His creations and best is to be interpreted as a maximal level of justice. There is no doubt that some cases of justice will yield unhappiness, so universes in which such instances occur may not appear in a multiverse where best equates to happiness, and vice-versa.

In the next case, once we have determined what "best" entails, we can look at various accounts of what particular beings or creations this concept ought to apply to.[14] That is to say, if we are to assume, for example, that best entails maximal happiness, then we need to determine to whom this happiness will apply.[15] Whether we take into account only humans when taking happiness into consideration, whether we include all sentient beings, plants, and so forth is the distinction that needs to be made. Just as is the case for the consequences of the various interpretations of what entails "best," the different interpretations of what creations this ought to apply to will result in a variety of different makeups of the multiverse. A multiverse in which we only take humans into consideration would have a very different composition than one in which we take both humans and other animals into account when looking at what is best for them. Again, this is because what is best for humans may not necessarily be what is best for all animals. This would result in varying numbers of universes being included in the multiverse, depending on the number of different creatures given consideration for what is best for them. The more creatures that we ought to give consideration to will require a more considerable number of universes within the multiverse in order to maximally satisfy them all. Furthermore, we will also need to consider whether this entailment of best applies to certain groups collectively or to each individual member of that group. For example, there may be a substantial difference in what is best for the collective human population versus what is best for me as an individual member of the human population. If I happen to be the carrier of some terribly infectious disease, then it may be best for the entire human population, or at least a decent portion of it, that I am quarantined and left to live out the rest of my life in isolation. Of course, this may not be the best thing for me, personally, since it would limit my freedom, happiness, and general well-being. So this is another level of that debate that will also have to be addressed and clarified.

What each of these distinctions and interpretations does for the theist is, essentially, establish a threshold below which, for them, no universe can be seen as plausible and therefore will not be included within the multiverse. So for the theists who believe that "best" entails a certain level of happiness within a particular universe, any universes that would not satisfy that minimal requirement would not be universes that can plausibly be part of the multiverse since it falls below the threshold set for inclusion. Similarly, if we are to consider only what is best for humans, all universes do not do what is best for humans could not be considered to be plausible parts of the multiverse. For example, one could suppose that, if we are working with the interpretation of "best for all creations" meaning "happiness for all humans," any universe that does not contain any humans would be precluded from being part of the multiverse.[16] So while the overall definition of omnibenevolence employed in my conception of God does not entail a threshold[17] for inclusion within the multiverse, various interpretations of this general definition will entail that a threshold is, or ought to be, established. Regardless of the specificities of the interpretation and where the threshold happens to appear, they will both be compatible with the overall account, and the defense of those specificities and the location of that threshold will remain the burden of the theist who forward those particular views.

There is a potential drawback, however, in accepting the account of omnibenevolence that I have given here. In accepting that omnibenevolence entails that God wants the best for all of His creations, this will, in some cases, commit the believer to skeptical theism. While I am not an opponent of skeptical theism, the fact remains that it is a controversial view within the philosophy of religion and for that reason the fact that this particular definition of omnibenevolence entails a certain level of skeptical theism can be seen as detrimental, to some. I will not engage in a discussion here about the overall plausibility of skeptical theism, except to say that it does play a role in this sense.[18] There are many instances in the world of states of affairs that seem to be bad, evil, and gratuitously evil. If we accept that God wants the best for all of His creations, then we will also have to accept that these evils are for the greater good of something, or that they simply do not matter and cannot aptly be classified as either good or evil, or with some other designation—they simply *are*. Whether this overall benefit or greater good appears within the particular universe itself or in some other universe within the multiverse, the theist will be forced to accept skeptical theism, face the problem of evil, or else provide some further alternative to account for the problem of evil.

OTHER ATTRIBUTES: OMNISCIENCE, TIMELESSNESS, IMMUTABILITY, AND NECESSITY

God's omniscience is typically taken to entail that He possesses knowledge of every true proposition and that since there are true propositions about not only what is the case but also about what could be the case, God's omniscience extends from the actual to the possible (Wierenga, 1989, p. 116). That is to say, "God knows not only what could happen and what will happen but also knows what would have happened if things had been different in various respects . . . God knows what free creatures would have done had they been in various alternative circumstances" (Wierenga, 1989, p. 117). Others have argued that this kind of propositional knowledge require that "(i) [proposition] p is true; (ii) [subject] S believes p; and (iii) S has adequate epistemic justification for believing p" (Hoffman and Rosenkrantz, 2002, p. 111). On this account, however, certain true propositions cannot be known by an omniscient being since they require a special kind of first-person access of the kind that an external omniscient being cannot have (Hoffman and Rosenkrantz, 2002, p. 112). An example of such a proposition may be something like "Deandre is thinking." Our subject, Deandre, can know that he is thinking, and an omniscient God can know that Deandre is thinking, but the argument is that Deandre may have a kind of knowledge about his thinking that is fundamentally of a different type than an omniscient God can have, as a result of his first-person access to this information. While this may or may not, in fact, be the case, the definition of omniscience that I employ moving forward is similar to the definition provided for omnipotence; namely, that God is omniscient in the sense that He knows all that it is possible for Him to know. As was the case for omnipotence this leaves it open for a wide variety of views on omniscience to be inserted here. Since the act of "knowing of," "knowing about," or "knowing that" does not seem to explicitly require any kind of direct causal relationship in the way of God acting on or in the natural world, it is not clear that there will be any significant compatibility issues between any account of omniscience and deism. It is for this reason that I am not wholly concerned about the nature of omniscience since it does not pose any direct concern with regards to direct divine intervention, which is the crux of our overall discussion.

Moving into a discussion of God's eternality or timelessness, Joshua Hoffman and Gary Rosenkrantz say that this can be understood in one of two ways; temporally or atemporally (2002, p. 97). In the first case, for God's timelessness to be understood temporally we can say that a being (x) has temporal eternity "if an only if (i) x exists at every time, and (ii) x has infinite temporal duration, and (iii) x has infinite temporal duration in both of the two temporal directions" (Hoffman and Rosenkrantz, 2002, p. 97). In the second case, of atemporal timelessness, we can say that being (x) "has atemporal eternity if and only if (i) x does not exist in time, and (ii) x is a necessary being" (Hoffman and Rosenkrantz, 2002, p. 97). From other perspectives, Edward Wierenga describes an eternal being as one who has "the complete possession all at once of illimitable life" (1989, p. 166), whereas the more popular conception of timelessness seems to be Nelson Pike's interpretation which claims that "[being] x is timeless if and only if x lacks temporal extension and x lacks temporal location" (1970, p. 7). Pike's definition seems to imply an atemporal conception of timelessness, and I am, admittedly, undecided on whether the conception that I would like to adopt for my deistic God is temporal or atemporal. The reason for this lack of preference is perhaps because there does not appear to be any substantial consequence or benefit in opting for one or the other in this case. Just as was the case with the various interpretations of omniscience it is not altogether clear that the overall account of a deistic God that I ultimately argue for is incompatible with either of these two strands of thought. With that said, I do have a tendency to prefer an account in which God is in time. The reason for this is because, as discussed by Wierenga (1989, p. 168), for an object or being to essentially possess an attribute He must possess it at every successive segment of time. An attribute X cannot be said to be essential to the object if there is a time T_1 where the object exists and possesses attribute X and a subsequent time T_2 where the object does not possess X. Similarly, to possess an attribute at all said attribute must be possessed by the object at some time T_1. If God is not in time and does not exist at any particular time segment, then He cannot possess any essential attributes, or attributes whatsoever, because He never has and will never exist at time T_1. To make such a claim regarding God is not one that I have much desire to do. So to argue that God is not within time is to add an extra set of considerations that ought to be dealt with, the above just being one example, and it is not entirely clear to me what the benefits of such a claim are. So, while the overall position that I put forth may be compatible with a God who is not in time, I do not think that such a step is warranted.

The particular conception of immutability that is adopted (or not) will be largely dependent on the conceptions of timelessness or eternality and omniscience that have been adopted to this point or will be adopted in the future. Returning to our example from above, if God is timeless and does not exist within time, then He does not exist at or in any particular segment of time. A change in an object can be characterized as the object having attribute X at time T_1 and then lacking attribute X at time T_2. Similarly, a change can be said to have occurred in an object if said object lacked attribute X at time T_1 but possessed attribute X at time T_2. For an object, God, in this case, to undergo change, it would have to minimally possess some attribute at a particular segment of time. Since a timeless God does not exist at any particular time segment, then He cannot be said to possess any attributes and thus cannot go through any changes. This is one sense in which we can view God as immutable or unchanging. As mentioned above, while the overall view that I have forwarded is consistent with this account, it is not one that I would particularly like to opt for, given the overall denial of God's possession of attributes. Again, for this reason, I will refrain from positing a particular kind of immutability (or lack thereof) in an attempt to maintain as open a conception of a deistic God as possible. With that in mind I do think that the most compatible and consistent route in this discussion is to argue for an immutable God, in the sense that given God's ultimate perfection, there is simply no need for Him to change in any regard at any point.

Finally, with regard to God's essentiality, I will not say much more than that, on the ontological view that I propose, He is essential. This simply entails that in our case, God necessarily exists in some sense with regard to the multiverse.[19]

THE ROLE THAT THESE ATTRIBUTES PLAY IN DEISM

It is not the most straightforward task to try to explain how each of these interpretations of the divine attributes, discussed in isolation from one another in conjunction with the adoption of a particular kind of multiverse theory entail a deistic God. It will often be the case that they will have to be discussed in relation to one another in order to make it clear just how deism follows as the most likely conclusion, and this becomes especially clear through the discussion of omnibenevolence, which has to be discussed only as it relates to omnipotence. Omnipotence, however, can generally be discussed on its own without having to appeal to any other divine attributes in order to show how it entails deism, but this will serve merely as a starting point. Again, while I do not discount the importance of the other divine attributes my discussion here will focus primarily on omnipotence and omnibenevolence, as there will not be enough time or space to devote detailed discussion to any of the other divine attributes. The hope is that through the discussion of omnipotence and omnibenevolence it will be rather clear how some of the other divine attributes can and will fit into the account and either entail deism or, minimally, be compatible with and pose no harm to the overall position of deism within the multiverse.

As we have seen, I have set out the definition of divine omnipotence to entail that God has the ability to do any task that is logically possible or that contains no self-contradiction, keeping in mind that some things that may be logically possible for us may be logically impossible in the context of actionable tasks for God (Mavrodes, 1963). Among these tasks, the most important and relevant ones for our purposes here will be the tasks of God doing something that is not within His nature—more specifically, acting in a less than perfectly efficient manner, or God acting in an arbitrary manner. For the sake of space, I will not recount the details of the discussions of these two types of action that has been provided above, and I will simply begin the discussion on how the aforementioned discussions factor into deism and the multiverse.

Given the structure of the multiverse and that it is comprised of any and all possible universes, any of God's action or intervention within it following the initial act of creation signifies a less than perfectly efficient way of bringing about some particular state of events. Being an all-powerful being, God not only could have actualized every possible universe in the multiverse but could have done so in the most efficient way possible—namely, in one single act. To call for a God who acts in the natural world, in any of the universes within the multiverse, throughout time is to claim that God was inefficient in His initial creation of the multiverse, and thus to deny either His omniscience or omnipotence, in some sense. To say that God acts throughout history is either to deny God's creative ability at the point of creation, such that He could not create things exactly as He so desired and has been relegated to making periodical amendments to His initial creation thus denying, or at least unnaturally limiting, His omnipotence. On the other hand, one could say that God needs to act in order to correct, guide, or restructure various happenings and goings-on within the multiverse, but this too poses problems, in that it places restrictions on God's omniscience.[20] To say that God is intervening in the natural order of things as a reaction to some particular event could be essentially to say that God is reacting to some particular event that He did not foresee and account for at the initial creation, which is clearly to deny

God of a certain level of knowledge. So in both cases in which we call for a God who acts within the natural order of things we call for a God who has severely retarded attributes of omnipotence and omniscience. If we are to maintain God's omnipotence, as I have defined it, as well as His omniscience and the notion that He would always act in the most efficient manner, then deism seems to be the only logical possibility. With intact omnipotence and omniscience God would have foreknown every possible outcome for every possible starting point of every universe, as well as had the power to create the initial starting points for every universe in such a way as to guarantee that they would realize only and all desired states of affairs across the spectrum of universes that He created to populate the multiverse. Finally, being a maximally efficient being, God would have done all of this in one single action, requiring no further intervention on His part, in that the most efficient way to bring something about is to do so with one single perfect act. For God to create everything that exists in one single act is not only the ultimate display of power but also the ultimate display of efficiency.

We have also discussed the notion of acting arbitrarily, and I have claimed that to make an arbitrary decision is not consistent with the nature of God since making arbitrary decisions are based on a lack of knowledge rather than a possession of knowledge. To say that God acts or has acted in an arbitrary manner is to deny Him some piece or pieces of knowledge that would allow Him to make an informed and motivated decision, and this would ultimately deny His omniscience. God would only act out of motivation. Whether it is possible that God can be motivated by anything external to Him is not of concern here, because whether He can or not, there still remains the ultimate motivation that would come from within Him, namely His will. So let us suppose that God is only motivated by His will (which I think is entirely plausible) before He would undertake any particular action His will would have to motivate Him to go forward with that action. In the absence of any will to do anything, it merely seems that God would refrain from acting. There is simply no motivation presented on or within God to take any particular course of action, so He remains idle, rather than just aimlessly undertaking various tasks just for the sake of undertaking them. To do so would be pointless, and something that we would expect more of a child or an imbecile than of a maximally powerful and all-knowing being.

Let us contextualize and situate this idea of motivated action within the multiverse. God, or anyone for that matter, acts for the sake of bringing about some possible state of affairs. Recall that the multiverse is comprised of a set of universes that, collectively, exhaust all possible states of affairs. For God to act within any particular universe to bring about some particular state of affairs would be problematic on two levels. The first is that, given the number of other universes that would have enjoyed the exact same historical past as whatever universe it is that God is about to act within, God would have to have made an arbitrary decision on which universe to act within. All things being equal, as they appear to be in this case, God ought to have no preference of acting on one universe rather than another, so we could say that He also has no motivation for action, thus entailing that He ought not to act on any universe at all. The second problem that arises is that every possible state of affairs is actualized at some place within the multiverse already, so the event that He aims to bring about via His intervention within a particular universe is already an event that would be occurring at the exact same time in the exact same context elsewhere in the multiverse. The only difference would be that in one universe it would occur via natural methods, while in the other one it would have come to pass via God's intervention. Again, it is not clear what would motivate God to desire to see the same set of events carried out at two different locations in the multiverse. In this sense, rather than remaining disconnected and allowing two distinct universes to carry on through the natural processes that He put in place (natural laws), His intervention would render two universes identical.[21] The decision to act on one of the universes to bring this about, once again, seems simply to be an arbitrary act based on nothing more than a desire to act for the sake of acting, something that it is not clear that God would be motivated to do in any sense.

The case of omnibenevolence is best discussed as a particular example of some of the tasks that have been discussed in relation to omnipotence. That is to say, the tasks or actions that have been discussed up to this point have been of a more general sense, whereas now we can further specify them as actions that display God's maximal love for His creations. So what can be said about actions that display God's omnibenevolence toward His creatures are really of no relevant difference to the types of actions that we have been discussing thus far, they are simply a subgroup within the broader definition of actions. The distinction between omnibenevolent actions and other God-actions, broadly construed, is of no significant difference here and I will continue on with an example to demonstrate this.[22]

Recall our fictional woman, Gillian, from chapter 3 who, in some universe within the multiverse, is trapped under a boulder that she cannot remove from herself. In this particular universe, call it U^1, there is no chance that anybody will come by to help Gillian. The boulder is so large that if it is not removed from Gillian within several minutes, she will go on to be crushed to death. We can also suppose that Gillian is, generally a good woman. She has not been perfect, but she also generally aims to help those around her and has committed no wildly terrible acts that resulted in a great deal of pain or suffering. So, this is the situation with which we are presented.

In such a situation, in a single-universe model, one would or at least could, possibly expect an omnibenevolent God to act to save Gillian from the pain and inevitable death with which she is faced. It would be effortless for God to lift the boulder off of Gillian in order to allow her to recover from her injuries and go on to live out the rest of her life. In the multiverse, however, we must remember that there are countless universes other than U^1 in which a counterpart of Gillian is in the same exact situation. Across this range of universes, every possible situation relating to the situation of Gillian (or a Gillian counterpart) is played out through natural processes not requiring the intervention of God. In some other universe, U^2, perhaps a counterpart of Gillian is aided by a passerby, whereas in some other universe, U^3, yet another counterpart of Gillian is able to fashion some sort of tool from nearby objects to help free herself, while in U^4 a Gillian counterpart dies suddenly after the boulder lands on her, and in U^5 a further Gillian counterpart receives no help, is unable to free herself, and dies a slow and painful death. Of course, these are only several examples of the possible courses of events that could come to play out with Gillian and her counterparts, but it goes to show that there is a wide range of possible outcomes that are all being actualized at some place within the multiverse. While for Gillian, in U^1, her situation is the only real situation and he may feel that an omnibenevolent God ought to help save him, this view is merely indexical. For God, all Gillian's and all of her counterparts across all of the universes are equally real. For God to act on Gillian would be to, as was discussed above, bring about a state of affairs that is already happening through natural processes elsewhere within the multiverse. No matter what course of action God takes, there will still remain countless universes in which Gillian or her counterparts are able to go on to live, as well as countless universes in which Gillian or her counterparts die from injuries related to being crushed by the boulder.

One possible way of getting around this problem of arbitrariness is to suggest that God's love for Gillian would act as a motivating factor, allowing God to act to save Gillian. But this response does not quite do the trick since God's love for Gillian is both maximal and equal to the love that He has for all of Gillian's counterparts across the multiverse. So, if He were to save Gillian in this one particular universe, then it would still be an arbitrary decision, because of the equality of His love for all Gillian's. Given that this is the case, it seems that God would have to make an arbitrary decision in which universe to save Gillian or her counterparts if that is something that is going to happen, and has already been argued, the idea of arbitrariness is not compatible with God. The best solution, in this case, would be to let the universes carry on as they would without any divine intervention and allow all possible realities to be realized across the multiverse.

CONCLUSION

The purpose of this chapter was to lay out some specifics of the nature of the deistic God that I argue for. In the first section, I provided some historical context of the nature of deism and some of the different conceptions of it that have been employed over time. I concluded that, given the overall lack of literature and lack of clarity as to the nature of God in that literature, the nature of the deistic God is one that is extremely vague and open to interpretation. Because of that, and for reasons of simplicity, I have opted to argue for a deistic God whose attributes do not vary drastically from those of the God of classical theism, save for several critical interpretations of those attributes. The next section contained a discussion of omnipotence as it relates to a deistic God, beginning my discussion on the overall nature of the deistic God. I opted for a kind of omnipotence similar to the kind that Mavrodes (1963) argues for in which His actions are limited to those permissible by logic and that there are some tasks that, while they contain no inherent contradiction within them, are not logically possible for God to perform. The inability to perform such tasks, however, is of no detriment to the doctrine of omnipotence. I went on to argue that, included among these tasks that are not logically possible for God to perform, are any tasks which are contrary to His nature and any tasks that require Him to perform with anything less than perfect efficiency. I then set out a broad definition of omnibenevolence and discussed some of the different possibilities that could play out given varying interpretations of what it means for God to want the best for His creations in the multiverse. In the next section, I discussed some considerations relating to God's omniscience, timelessness, immutability, and necessity. Again, I intentionally left the general interpretation of these attributes open so as to allow for an inclusive account, because it is not clear that any particular reasonable interpretation of any of these attributes is wholly incompatible with multiverse deism. And, finally, I discussed how all of these attributes, together with one another, come together to play into the overall nature of a deistic God of the multiverse. This section allowed us to see a more full-fledged idea of the kind of God that I propose, rather than a segmented view as was presented in the previous sections.

NOTES

1. A significant number of writings on deism have to do more with the politics of being a proponent of deism rather than of the view itself. Still, some information on deistic ideals can be found in Byrne (1989) and Leland (1755).

2. Kenny (1979), Pojman (2001), Rowe (2007), Wainwright (1987) to name a few volumes with substantial sections on divine attributes.

3. Deists were often deemed atheists by the church and state.

4. This and many other definitions of deism will often include something detailing the ability to know of God's existence through reason alone. I do not make such a claim. I am only concerned with God's inactiveness in the world, and not how we are to come about believing that He exists.

5. By this I mean to include pantheism, panentheism, or any other conception of God.

6. These, too, are not altogether clear, but for the present purposes they would simply call for the existence of God, for Him to be the creator, and that He refrains from intervening in the natural order of the world after the initial act of creation.

7. It has been argued that creating a stone so heavy that He cannot lift it is logically impossible for God, given His nature, even though there is no inherent contradiction within the task. This will be discussed further, shortly.

8. Forrest (2012) discusses some of the potential motivating factors or "tie-breakers" in these kinds of situations.

9. Here it is important to make the distinction that the act of making a decision can be motivated or guided but not the act of making a decision in favor of a particular outcome.

10. There is also the thought that making an arbitrary decision can be based on the possession of too much knowledge, but this is a claim that I disagree with, for reasons that I will not get into here. To mount a detailed discussion of the nature of arbitrariness would be tangential to the current discussion, so I will just move forward with the assumption that an arbitrary decision is based on a lack of knowledge. Forrest (2012) writes about this as it relates to Buridan's Ass.

11. "Inability," in this sense, can also be equated to "lack of desire" since anything that God wills is done.

12. If we are to limit the evaluation of power to the production of the highest quality philosophy, and we are in a position in which we have to decide which young man is more powerful.

13. While God acting would directly bring about an event, E1, in one sense, it is indirect in the sense that it is an external force coming in to change the natural course of events that could still have brought about E1.

14. Aristotle (1998) discusses a similar issue in Book IV of *The Nicomachean Ethics* when discussing prodigality and to whom it applies.

15. The complexities involved in determining this can be seen in ethics, especially in the discussion of animal rights.

16. Barring some sort of view where existence is not a necessary condition of happiness.

17. Or at least, if it does, it is extremely low.

18. See Dougherty & McBrayer (2014), Johnson (2013), Snapper (2011) and Hasker (2010) for some recent discussion, both for and against, skeptical theism.

19. More discussion on the necessity of God will come in chapter 7.

20. This could carry on into a full-fledged discussion of free-will and determinism, but it is beyond the scope of this paper to investigate and discuss the compatibility of omniscience and free-will. I am aware of this issue, though.

21. Identical with regard to their states of affairs, but perhaps not their causal chains that led to those states of affairs.

22. More will also be said about omnibenevolent actions in the next chapter in the discussion on divine hiddenness.

Chapter 5

Why Being a Deist May Not Be So Bad

Up to this point, I have tried to show how the acceptance of a certain kind of multiverse theory, along with the desire to maintain the existence of God, entails the existence of a deistic God rather than the God of classical theism. While I have made the case for an entailment that is logically consistent, I have done little to show why such an alternative to classical theism might be beneficial or preferred over the God of classical theism. The deistic conception of God is one that has been largely dismissed for the past several centuries and has been largely omitted from contemporary discussions of plausible alternatives to classical theism in a subfield of philosophy of religion that is rapidly expanding. The current attitude and outlook on deism however, I believe, is due to its dismissal by many thinkers several hundred years ago. I also think that a new look at the overall conception with fresh eyes and mind is needed not only to legitimately evaluate the plausibility of such an account but also to assess the potential benefits or deficiencies of it given the current state of philosophical and theological discourse. Given the virtual nonexistence of deism within the academic philosophical and theological discussions, it is apparent that deism carries with it some sort of negative connotation or idea of implausibility. I believe that, if this is the case, it is unfairly so. With the recent influx of new arguments both for and against atheism, there is now a chance to take a more in-depth look at the viability of deistic thought within the overall context of the philosophy of religion. As we have already seen that deism seems to be a better fit with certain multiverse theories than classical theism is we can now move on to explore how deism holds up against some of these contemporary arguments for atheism. We can also look at whether or not deism fares better against these arguments for atheism than classical theism does, and whether or not deism is compatible with some of the common arguments for theism.

In the first half of this chapter, several arguments for the existence of God will be discussed in order to show that a deistic conception of God is compatible with teleological arguments, ontological arguments, and cosmological arguments. In the second half of this chapter, there will be a look at several of the stronger and more well-known contemporary arguments against God's existence that may pose problems for the classical theistic conception of God: the argument from divine hiddenness, the problem of evil, and some problems surrounding the issue of miracles. Finally, the last section discusses how a generic deistic conception of God may be able to get around some of the difficulties that classical theism faces in dealing with these atheistic arguments and shows that deism may be able to respond to some of these atheistic arguments adequately. Before moving forward, I will note that the brand of deism that I will be referring to in this chapter is a generic one,[1] which simply entails that God is not active in the natural world. This generic conception contains no explanation or specifications as to how or why God is not active; it merely puts forth that He is not. The reason for this is to show that, while a simple deistic account is not only compatible with arguments for God's existence and though it may also be able to provide a better response to some atheistic arguments than classical theism can, it is simply a move in the right direction and it cannot go all the way in addressing some of the issues that are raised by each specific argument. So, this generic deism will serve as a starting or reference point for varying deistic accounts that will all, in principle, be able to stand up to various atheistic arguments yet still be compatible with common theistic arguments in their own specialized ways. Specific versions of each argument for or against atheism will, for the most part, not be discussed here; rather, general families of kinds of arguments will be addressed. That is to say, arguments from divine hiddenness will be discussed as a whole without narrowing the focus on one particular version of the argument from divine hiddenness. Likewise, the group of arguments for atheism that deal with miracles and divine intervention will be discussed, and so too will arguments that deal with the problem of evil. In some cases, specific arguments will be mentioned but this is only done in the event that that particular argument can generally be taken to be a paradigm case of what the remainder of the arguments in that family aim to show, and it will serve both time and space simply to discuss that particular argument in a general sense.

ARGUMENTS FOR GOD'S EXISTENCE

It is important to note that my aim here is not to conduct an investigation into or evaluation of whether or not these theistic arguments are ultimately successful in arguing for God's existence. It is quite possible that some or all of these arguments are ultimately unsuccessful, or at least unconvincing, and that is fine, for my purposes here. My aim here is solely to show that if these arguments are successful, then they motivate deism, minimally, as much as they motivate theism, if not more.

TELEOLOGICAL ARGUMENTS

Teleological arguments are empirical, bottom-up arguments that can vary in form but which generally aim to show that some or all objects in nature appear to be objects of intelligent design, and then inferring that this intelligent designer is God. Typically, teleological arguments utilize reasoning from seemingly intentionally structured features of the observable world to the existence of one or more supernatural designer(s) (Manson, 2003, p. 1). Similarly, a proponent of the teleological argument will often argue that multiple phenomena in nature display such intricacy in terms of overall structure, function and/or interconnectedness with other phenomena that to view these processes as a result of deliberate design is simply natural, if not altogether inescapable . . . and this deliberate design is typically taken to be supernatural, and prior to nature (Ratzsch, 2010) essentially making the claim that, rather than individual aspects of nature, nature in its entirety appears to be an object of intelligent design. Since the designer of an object must be an entity external and prior to it, the designer must be a God-like entity. Arguments of this family

> begin with a . . . specialized catalogue of properties and end with a conclusion concerning the existence of a designer with the *intellectual* properties (knowledge, purpose, understanding, foresight, wisdom, intention) necessary to *design* the things exhibiting the special properties in question. With that in mind, however, these kinds of arguments do not typically reason directly to God as the creator, so other, additional, arguments are needed in order to make that step. (Manson, 2003, p. 1)

In broad outline, then, teleological arguments focus upon finding and identifying various traces of the operation of a mind in nature's temporal and physical structures, behaviors and paths" (Ratzsch, 2010).

There are several ways by which the theist is able to go about making his teleological argument. Dal Ratzsch subdivides the teleological family of arguments into three different *Schemas* into which particular arguments within the family will fall (Ratzsch, 2010). In the first case, which we can call, *Schema 1*, it is a simple analogical argument in which one object in nature appears to be similar in some relevant way to another object that we know is the product of intelligent design, therefore, it is reasonable to infer that both objects are products of intelligent design. In the second case, *Schema 2*, the teleologian makes a similar, yet different, claim regarding the origin of design-like objects found in nature. He argues that the occurrence of design-like or higher-order properties cannot come about from non-intentional, natural processes. This version of the argument is not to say, however, that higher-order cognition and design-like properties found within nature cannot be seen as products of natural processes, but that if this is the case, then it is the natural processes themselves which are products of intentional design. And finally, in *Schema 3*, an inference to best explanation is employed to explain the appearance of intelligent design in nature. In this last case, the teleologian draws a connection between the apparent design-like features of various aspects of nature and the assumption that the best explanation for these design-like features is intentional design. Because the best explanation for the design-like features of nature is the act of intentional design, we are justified in believing that there exists a designer.

Similarly, Neil Manson differentiates between design[2] and cosmological arguments[3] within the family of teleological arguments. He argues that, while both types rely on *a posteriori* premises to forward their claims, cosmological arguments rely on premises that are "highly general and apparently incorrigible" (Manson, 2003, p. 2) when compared to those premises utilized by design arguments. Premises in design arguments tend to pluck out much more specific aspects of the observable world and use them to make the case for an intelligent designer. Elliot Sober goes on to further differentiate between different types of design arguments, classifying them as either organismic design arguments or cosmic design arguments (Sober, 2003, p. 27). With that classification in place, however, he still goes on to note that the thread common to all design arguments "is that design describe some empirical feature of the world and argue that this feature points towards an explanation in terms of God's intentional planning and away from an explanation in terms of mindless natural processes" (Sober, 2003, p. 27).

In each of the various cases of teleological arguments discussed above, it does not seem evident that there are any contradictions or inconsistencies if we are to frame them with a generic deistic conception of God. In fact, each schema presented by Ratzsch or subgroup differentiated between by Manson or Sober that has been presented seems to be perfectly compatible with a deistic conception of God. Because each schema and subgroup makes claims regarding only the origin of objects in nature or, more importantly, regarding the origin of nature itself rather than on any present or future divine interactions within nature they all seem perfectly in-tune with deism. None of the versions of teleological arguments presented above is concerned explicitly with any continued supernatural presence or activity within nature; rather, each is principally concerned with the primary cause or creation of various objects within nature or of nature itself. So too is deism. This means that any teleological argument either already is or can be reduced to, a version that is compatible with a deistic conception of God.

In addition to teleological arguments being compatible with deism, it is also possible that they work better with multiverse theories than they do with single-universe theories when it comes to making the case for the existence of God. Given that the proponent of teleological arguments will typically argue that the complexity of our universe infers a designer, it could be argued that the multiverse (since it, necessarily, contains more than one universe) is exponentially, and possibly infinitely, more complex than any single universe. Such an increased level of complexity surely points toward the existence of a designer just as much, if not more, than any single-universe model. And then, of course, the argument that this designer is God will have to be made in addition. So while some may see the multiverse as undercutting some of the strength of teleological arguments, it is also a viable option to see the multiverse as the perfect fit for teleological arguments.

ONTOLOGICAL ARGUMENTS

Ontological arguments argue for the conclusion that God exists through the use of premises that are derived from sources other than external observation. That is to say, ontological arguments are composed of analytic, *a priori*, necessary premises that all lead to the conclusion that God exists. Dating back to the eleventh century when an argument of this type first appeared in Anselm's *Proslogion*, other philosophers such as Descartes, Aquinas, Hume, Kant, Hegel, and Plantinga have followed suit and gone on to advance their own unique ontological arguments.[4] To show the myriad of different kinds of arguments that fall under the umbrella of the ontological argument family, Graham Oppy (1995) differentiates between eight different types of ontological arguments. While I will not go into detail describing what each of these differentiations specifically entails, the list itself illustrates that the family of ontological arguments is broad enough to include definitional ontological arguments; conceptual (or hyperintensional) ontological arguments; modal ontological arguments; Meinongian ontological arguments; experiential ontological arguments; mereological ontological arguments; higher-order ontological arguments; and "Hegelian" ontological arguments.

While not quite easily defined, ontological arguments generally rely on *a priori* knowledge or claims that are used to argue for God's existence. Because of the *a priori* nature of the wide variety of ontological arguments, that do not rely on any "real world" evidence, it is not evident that there is any tension between arguments of this sort (generally) and deism. The more common ontological arguments tend to be definitional or conceptual, so while there may be specific instances where a particular ontological argument may seem to be incompatible with deism, these incompatibilities will not be clear-cut and will generally be able to be argued as being reduced to questions of semantics and definitions. While there is the possibility of particular ontological arguments being formulated that are not compatible with deism (i.e., one that argues that God is a supremely perfect being, that being causally connected to and active within the natural world is a perfection, therefore God ought to be causally connected to and active within the natural world), these are merely specified cases of an ontological argument. In a case such as this, the incompatibility only arises due to a particular interpretation of what exactly it is that perfection entails. It will only be on specific interpretations of this term that an inconsistency will arise, meaning that it is not the structure or type of the argument as a whole that is not compatible with deism, rather it is in a definitional interpretation of that argument that leads to the apparent incompatibility. It is possible for deism to be incompatible with particular instances of the ontological argument, but that does not entail incompatibility with the family of arguments as a whole. And in cases where there is an incompatibility between deism and a particular version of an ontological argument then this, at worst, renders deism on-par with classical theism, since they both will require further explanation and justification in terms of defining and conceiving of the divine attributes.

COSMOLOGICAL ARGUMENTS

As is the case for ontological arguments, cosmological arguments are less a particular argument than they are a type of argument, and they have recently shown a tremendous resurgence within the philosophy of religion (Nowacki, 2007, p. 14). Cosmological arguments, as briefly mentioned in the discussion of teleological arguments, use a general pattern of argumentation that infers the existence of God from certain alleged facts about the natural world (Reichenbach, 2012). Some of these initial alleged facts are that (1) the universe, or at least various aspects of it, is contingent and/or causally dependent, (2) that certain events and beings in the universe are contingent, and (3) that the universe came into being at some point. From these facts, the proponent of the cosmological argument will infer, deductively, inductively, abductively, or by inference to the best explanation that God exists (Reichenbach, 2012).

As we saw with ontological arguments and teleological arguments, cosmological arguments can be further divided up into subgroups, a task that was undertaken by William Lane Craig in 1980. Craig argues that cosmological arguments fall into one of three categories; (1) those based on the impossibility of an essentially ordered infinite regress, (2) those that argue that an infinite temporal regress is impossible because an actual infinite is impossible (which he calls the *kalam* argument), and (3) any cosmological argument that is based on the Principle of Sufficient Reason (Craig, 1980, p. 282). In the first case, an argument based on the argument for the impossibility of an essentially ordered infinite regress would look something like this:

1. A contingent being (a being such that if it exists, it could have not-existed or could cease to) exists.
2. This contingent being has a cause of or explanation for its existence.
3. The cause of or explanation for its existence is something other than the contingent being itself.
4. What causes or explains the existence of this contingent being must either be solely other contingent beings or include a noncontingent (necessary) being.
5. Contingent beings alone cannot provide an adequate causal account or explanation for the existence of a contingent being.
6. Therefore, what causes or explains the existence of this contingent being must include a noncontingent (necessary) being.
7. Therefore, a necessary being (a being such that if it exists cannot not-exist) exists (Reichenbach, 2012).

An example of the second case, the *kalam* argument,[5] would be something along the lines of:

1. Everything that begins to exist has a cause of its existence.
2. The universe began to exist.
3. Therefore, the universe has a cause of its existence.
4. Since no scientific explanation (in terms of physical laws) can provide a causal account of the origin of the universe, the cause must be personal (explanation is given in terms of a personal agent) (Reichenbach, 2012).

It is easy to note that in the first case there is a denial of the possibility of an actual infinite, whereas in the second case the primary concern is of the temporal nature of the explanation of the universe. Finally, in the third case, an argument based on the Principle of Sufficient Reason can be seen, arguing that there is generally a simple explanation behind everything. That is to say that if something unexplained is to occur, then the explanation for that occurrence is likely the simplest plausible explanation rather than some other overtly complex option. Since the complexity of the universe is unimaginably high, and so too would be the scientific explanation of the origin and creation of that universe, we ought to look at the far more simple, theistic account of the origin of the universe as our explanation.

Cosmological arguments as a whole generally tend to argue for an initial cause or explanation for the existence of the universe or some phenomena within the universe. In that, cosmological arguments generally do not tend to make claims regarding the ongoing nature of the universe, save for the fact that the universe functions in a particular way because of the will of some willful designer. Very few, if any, cosmological arguments make claims regarding the ongoing causal connection and activity of a creating being within the universe, leaving the primary concern of the argument to be the origin or explanation of the universe. In this, cosmological arguments are largely compatible with deism and are perhaps the most obviously compatible with deism out of the three kinds of arguments for theism that have been discussed thus far. The reason for this is that both deism and cosmological arguments are concerned primarily with the initial cause of the universe, with both tending not to make any further substantial claims regarding the ongoing operation and continued sustenance of that universe.

ARGUMENTS AGAINST GOD'S EXISTENCE

It is important to note that my aim here, as was the case with the arguments for God's existence, is not to conduct an investigation into or evaluation of whether or not any these particular arguments are ultimately successful. It is quite possible that some or all of these arguments are ultimately unsuccessful, or at least unconvincing, and that is fine, for my purposes here. My aim here is solely to show that if these arguments are successful, then they are just as damaging, if not more, to theism as they are to deism. As such, the deist fares no worse than the theist in terms of responding to these potential arguments.

DIVINE HIDDENNESS

There is a range of different versions of arguments for atheism from divine hiddenness, each with their own unique details and subtleties. The common thread that runs through all of them, however, is that God is absent from our lives and the world in ways that we should not expect Him to be, and because of that absence, or *hiddenness*, we can infer God's nonexistence.

One particular version of the argument for atheism from divine hiddenness argues that holding a personal relationship with God is the greatest possible good and that since God is omnibenevolent, He should always want the best for all of His creatures, but that many of us who desire a personal relationship with God do not have one. Therefore, since God is not present to actualize this greatest of all goods, then He surely is not all-loving, and in fact, does not exist. That is to say, in being absent from people's lives in this respect, God is not exemplifying His omnibenevolence, which means that He, as classical Judeo-Christian monotheism describes Him, does not exist.

One of the most well-known arguments for atheism from divine hiddenness comes from J. L. Schellenberg's 2004 essay "Divine Hiddenness Justifies Atheism." The argument put forth by Schellenberg in this essay is that God is hidden from us in that we are witness to "the absence of convincing evidence for the existence of God, or, more specifically, to the absence of some kind of positive experiential result in the search for God" (Schellenberg, 2004, p. 31), which leads us to the conclusion that we are justified in holding reasonable nonbelief in the existence of God. That is to say, there are numerous people who seek out some sort of interactive experience with God, be it simply some sort of communication or validation, a healing or helping hand, or some other sort of revelation, but these kinds of interactions between God and those who desire them are all too often nonexistent. If it is the case that there exists a God who has the power and desire to maximize happiness for all of His creatures, God as described by classical theism, then we would not be able to reasonably expect the kind of absence of God that we do see given certain situations. Because we do see such an absence in areas where we would reasonably expect an omnibenevolent and omnipotent God to act, then Schellenberg argues that we are justified in believing in the nonexistence of the classical theistic God. Furthermore, this is precisely the kind of justified non-belief that God would not allow, and definitely not allow in such prevalence, so this provides us with one more reason for suspecting that He does not exist.

While this kind of argument may pose problems for the classical theistic conception of God, a deistic conception of God will not face those same issues. Since a deistic God plays no ongoing causal role within the world, it cannot be expected of Him to continuously create or maintain reciprocal personal relationships with His creatures. Classical theism argues for a personal God who has interaction not only within the natural world but with us as well, but deism is explicit in its denial of such interactions. For this reason, an absence of God's knowable activity may pose some problems and raise questions for a classical theistic conception, whereas the same cannot be said for a deistic conception. Arguments such as Schellenberg's are structured in a way as to derive reasonable nonbelief from a lack of displayed divine characteristics that ought to be readily observable to us. More specifically, divine intervention by way of fostering loving and personal relationships with those who desire them. In a deistic conception of God, the possibility of causal interaction from God is not expected and is, in fact, precluded, so to mount an argument for atheism, or at least for reasonable nonbelief in the existence of God, based on a lack of such interaction does nothing to harm deism. In a case such as this, when applying a Schellenberg-type argument to any deistic account of God, the argument does no damage in that it is trying to justify reasonable nonbelief based on the absence of an expected behavior which is explicitly denied by that particular conception of God. It is almost akin to criticizing a human for not being able to breathe underwater. It is not something that we would expect of him in any circumstance, so to criticize him based on the absence of his ability to breathe underwater does no harm to him, just as the argument from divine hiddenness does no direct harm to a deistic conception of God. Even on weaker versions of deism, such as epistemic deism,[6] God would still be "hidden" from us in that His work would not be epistemically accessible to us, so an argument from divine hiddenness of this sort would not harm this version of deism, nor would it harm a stronger version of deism where God's causal interaction within the natural world is not a metaphysical possibility.

Although Schellenberg's argument is often taken to exemplify the argument from divine hiddenness, other types that do not explicitly call for the kind of divine intervention seemingly required by Schellenberg's argument may pose more of a problem for multiverse deism. In another type of argument from divine hiddenness, one might argue that while direct divine intervention should not be expected, we should expect that if God exists, we should all have a clearer picture in our minds of His nature and the overall type of being that He is. Since we do not have consensus at all on what God's nature is or what type of being He is, He does not exist because such a powerful and loving being would not allow us to be in such darkness regarding His nature, and He surely would not allow people to hold the belief that He does not exist. Similarly, the argument could come based on morality, arguing that the key to living a good and meaningful life comes from living a morally good life and that moral prescriptions come from God. But there is great debate about the nature of morality, and if God existed, He surely would not allow for such murkiness in understanding such a crucial issue. In response to these types of arguments from divine hiddenness the multiverse deist could respond by claiming that we simply happen to be in a universe in which we do not have a clear picture of God's nature, or morality, but that there are other universes in the multiverse in which their inhabitants do have clarity on such issues. It could very well be the case that inhabitants of other universes have their minds composed in such a way as to be born with, or come to develop clear, concise and unified views into the true nature of God or morality. We just happen to be in a universe in which we do not have those capacities. Of course, whether such alternatives are possible or plausible will vary depending on different conceptions of multiverse construction, but this is simply one possible response that the multiverse deist can give. In cases such as this, the multiverse deist will often be able to appeal to responses that appeal to the indexical nature of our universe, and to the logical possibility, or necessity, of the existence of other universes where things are other than they are in ours.

While the kinds of weaknesses that arguments from divine hiddenness point out in classical theism do not translate and apply directly to deism, some other difficulties with deistic theories come to light. In this case, even if a deistic God does not reveal Himself to us occasionally, then perhaps the advocate of the argument from hiddenness is justified in asking how come God did not create a universe in which His existence is manifest to us, or at least more obvious to us, in some way other than direct divine interventions, but we have seen how the multiverse deist may go about responding to such an argument.[7] Arguments from hiddenness could also cast a shadow of doubt on the supposed omnipotent, omnibenevolent, and omniscient nature of God, and so the deist would have to do some work in explaining if and how these divine attributes are to be maintained in a world in which God does not have any occasion to demonstrate these qualities. Furthermore, if it is not the case that God exemplifies these omni-qualities, then the deist must also show how it is the case that He is, in fact, a God rather than, at best, a natural process or cause of the universe. So it does not seem that Schellenberg-type arguments from divine hiddenness pose any substantial threat to the multiverse deist, but other types of arguments from divine hiddenness may, minimally, cause the multiverse deist to provide an added level of explanation as to why the existence of God, or some aspect of Him, is not clearly available to us. On this, the multiverse deist at least calls for the proponent of arguments from divine hiddenness to reframe his argument to attack to the specific account of the multiverse with which he is working. The requirement to reframe the argument is already more than classical theism requires of arguments from divine hiddenness, so it seems that multiverse deism is preferential to classical theism in such cases.

THE PROBLEM OF EVIL

Often similar to arguments from divine hiddenness (Schellenberg, 2006), both in the argument itself and in the nature of the response that can be given by the deist, are arguments from evil. Arguments of this kind try to point out that there seems to be a great deal of gratuitous evil, harm, and pain in the world that is caused through both the actions of other creatures and natural processes of the world.[8] The argument sets out to make the point that if a God existed who was truly omnipotent, omniscient, and omnibenevolent then these evils would not exist, for a God who exemplified all of these attributes would surely either prevent all of these gratuitous evils from occurring or not allow all of these to continuously happen (Dougherty, 2011, p. 563). Essentially, arguments from the problem of evil tend to cast doubt on one or more of the divine attributes, arguing that God must be ignorant of the evils that we endure (aimed at omniscience), that He does not have adequate power to stop these evils (aimed at omnipotence), or that He simply is disinterested in stopping them (aimed at omnibenevolence). J. L. Mackie summarizes the problem in saying that "In its simplest form the problem of evil is this: God is omnipotent; God is wholly good; and yet evil exists. There seems to be some contradiction between these three propositions, so that if any two of them were true the third would be false" (Mackie, 1978, p. 18).[9] In response to arguments of this type the classical theist must somehow convince us that all of the aforementioned divine attributes can be maintained while at the same time allowing for the apparent abundance of gratuitous evils that we see in the world, or else deny the claim that there exist gratuitous evils in the world and that there is some greater good that must come from all of the sufferings that we see and experience. M. B. Ahern speaks of the theistic solution to the problem of evil in saying that "[t]here are certain ways in which theists can avoid the problems of evil. They can be avoided by giving certain accounts of God's power or goodness. . . . In each case, however, there is a price for theists to pay" (1971, p. x). He goes on to say that almost every theistic response to the problem of evil carries with them the "cost of rejecting the usual Christian and Judaistic concept of God" (Ahern, 1971, p. xi). The adoption of multiverse deism is a perfect example of the rejection of the traditional God that Ahern speaks of.

Arguments from the problem of evil can be further differentiated between and categorized into either evidential arguments from evil or logical arguments from evil, with the aforementioned Mackie and Ahearn exemplifying the logical arguments from evil.[10] In either case, the classical theistic conception of God is attacked on the grounds that there are gratuitous evils that occur and that the existence of such gratuitous evils is incompatible with the existence of God, as He is traditionally conceived. Where logical arguments will refer to evil in a broad sense,[11] not picking out any specific evil in particular, like the needlessly suffering fawn described by William Rowe (1979),[12] to demonstrate how its existence is incompatible with the existence of God, the evidential arguments[13] will pick out specific instances of evil and try to demonstrate how the existence of that particular evil instance is not compatible with the existence of God.

For the multiverse deist, the evidential problem of evil does not directly pose much of a problem since it primarily attacks God based on His either allowing or failing to prevent a significant number of the gratuitous evils that we see or experience. These two points of attack that could be areas of difficulty for the classical theist are not for the deist, since the two aspects referred to by the proponent of the argument from evil, allowing and/or failing to prevent evil acts, are both actions required of God in the natural world, which are precluded by deism. Even in the sense in which the action terms are used here would require a passive activity by God, which is activity nonetheless. Evils in the world are either caused by God or else allowed by God through His permitting processes that lead to moral and natural evils (allowing free will, allowing natural laws to operate in certain ways, etc.). Many theists would deny the possibility that God could explicitly cause the evils that we see in the world, but that still leaves them vulnerable to the arguments that stem from God permitting (rather than actualizing) evil in the world. The deistic account, however, does a better job in dealing with the argument from the permission of evil than the classical theist does because, again, permitting something seems to entail that God is taking an active role in the world and that is explicitly precluded. Because of this, from the deistic perspective, we cannot expect that God would either allow or fail to prevent any kinds of evil that we may experience in our world because either one of those two options would entail God's activity. In the case of the logical problem of evil, however, the multiverse deist may face more challenging circumstances due to the more broad nature of the particular arguments that fall under it. That is, when employing a logical argument from evil, there need not be reference to a particular actual or potential example of gratuitous evil in order for the argument to work, so the multiverse deist will not be able to simply respond to that one particular example, rather he will have to respond to a more general and abstract argument attacking the overall nature of God and its compatibility with certain states of affairs. With that said, however, multiverse deism is still able to avail itself of more potential responses to logical arguments from evil than can the classical conception of God in a single-universe model. In either case, the multiverse deist will, at the very least, fare no worse than the classical theist when confronted by logical arguments from the problem of evil, and he still holds the opportunity to offer superior and more varied responses than classical theism can.

While the divine activity (or lack thereof) perspective of the problem of evil proves not to be a very damaging argument against the deist, there are still aspects of the argument that will need to be addressed. As is a problem that the classical theist has to face, the presence of gratuitous evils in the world seems to be inconsistent with one or more of God's omnipotence, omniscience and omnibenevolence, from the deistic perspective. Despite the fact that the deist argues that we cannot expect God to act to stop the occurrences of these evils, the above divine attributes can still be questioned by arguing that if God is the creator of the universe or multiverse, whether He is active in it today or not, if these divine attributes are to be exemplified then

God would have known how to, have been able to, would have desired to, and would indeed have created a world in which none of these gratuitous evils exist. The multiverse deist, however, is not limited to providing responses from the deistic perspective but he can also avail himself of a number of responses that stem from the multiverse aspect of his ontological view, by arguing that evil events are metaphysically possible and thus are necessarily instantiated within the multiverse, for example, which is something that the proponent of a single-universe model cannot appeal to. So, in addition to any deistic responses to the problem of evil, other responses appealing to a greatness in variety of kinds of universes, certain indexicality arguments regarding our universe, and the like can be provided instead of or in conjunction with any of the deistic responses provided. This deistic amendment to the problem of evil still, however, leaves the deist with some questions to answer regarding the existence of evil and its apparent incompatibility with three of the divine attributes, or whether or not these three divine attributes are even exemplified by God, and if so, to what extent.

ISSUES WITH MIRACLES

Miracles and divine intervention are often appealed to by classical theists as evidence for the existence of their God however various aspects of reports of miracles, religious experiences, and divine intervention have been scrutinized and employed as different arguments against the existence of God. Various aspects of divine intervention are used to highlight supposed inconsistencies or weaknesses within the classical theist's account of either particular religious experiences or religious experiences as a whole. One hurdle that theists must overcome is that, when arguing for the veridicality of a miracle,[14] the theist must prove not only that the particular law or laws of nature in operation are, in fact, operational laws of nature, but also that this law has actually been broken by this miraculous act which took place. These seem to be two contradictory tasks that must co-exist with each other, posing a problem for proponents of miracles. If an event such as a miracle occurs, then the supposed natural laws were not the real laws working, the earlier state was not as it was supposed to be, or the system was not closed, meaning that the supposed miraculous event did not actually break the supposed or purported relevant law of nature. The stronger the law of nature is, the more improbable an event contrary to it would be, thus giving it maximal improbability, in turn, rendering it a miracle.[15] It is this maximal improbability that makes the event miraculous, but it is also this maximal improbability that the testimony or perception of the event in question must overcome (Mackie, 1982, pp. 21–25). That is to say, the presence of the laws of nature discount any reports or even experiences of a miracle, while the occurrence of a miracle discounts the strength of the relevant laws of nature, and for any event to be deemed a true miracle it requires that neither of these two things be discounted in any way, posing problems for the proponent of miracles. That is to say, for an event to be a miracle not only must the law of nature be guaranteed wholly, but so too must the event that violated that law of nature.

One of the more well-known arguments regarding miracles is that of David Hume (1985), which argues that we ought to proportion our belief to the amount and quality of the evidence, and that since our evidence that suggests that miracles do not occur is far stronger, in both respects, than our evidence that suggests that miracles do occur, we are not justified in believing that miracles occur.[16] That is to say, throughout our lives, we continuously experience things that reinforce our understanding of natural laws, and that we have an enormously large amount of instances and experiences that we have already experienced that are in accordance with, and reaffirm, those beliefs. A miracle, or event which seems to break a natural law, would be only a one-time counterexample of these natural laws. Because of the sheer volume of instances that confirm that natural laws are in operation and cannot be broken, we ought to believe that these natural laws cannot be broken. We cannot change our belief system of the way the natural world operates simply because of one potential counterexample, and we must hold onto our beliefs that carry a large amount of justification with them. While Hume's argument does not explicitly argue against the occurrence of miracles, it argues against our ability to hold reasonable justification that miracles occur. An argument such as this poses problems for classical theism because much of classical theism is based on the occurrence of miracles. Miraculous events play a significant role in the historical aspects of classical theism, in that many religions come to be based on some sort of revelation at the beginning, the subsequent scripture is often based on or includes a variety of different revelations and miraculous events. Miracles thus play a significant role in both maintaining old and attracting new followers to particular faiths.

A final common issue that can be raised regarding miracles and divine intervention is that different revelations are often claimed by various religions and belief-systems, each of which argues that one or more particular revelations give credence to the "truth" of their religion. This poses a problem because there are a number of different religions that all claim to be the one and only true religion, and the evidence that each religion cites for such claims is all of the same type. That is to say, religion A will argue that revelation A^1 proves that religion A is the true religion, while at the same time religion B will argue that revelation B^2 proves that religion B is the true religion. Simultaneously, religion A will argue that revelation B^2 ought to be discounted and provides no evidence for the truth of religion B, whereas religion B will argue that revelation A[1] ought to be discounted and provides no evidence for the truth of religion A. One employing the argument of miraculous incompatibility would argue that since there are a variety of miracles and revelations that all seem to point at various incompatible truths, and we have no way of determining which of these truths is "right," we ought to discount the evidential value of all of them.

Each of the above arguments for atheism that deal with revelations and miracles poses problems for the traditional theistic account of God and His action within the natural world. While they may not prove to be knock-down arguments, they certainly raise certain issues and inconsistencies that ought to be resolved in the traditional theistic account of God. These issues, however, are not issues that will have to be faced by the kind of multiverse deistic account that I propose, nor are they issues that will need to be reconciled in any sense by the deist. This is because of the nature of the multiverse model that I have argued for, in which any divine intervention would be superfluous and unnecessary as well as because of the nature of deism, as I have described it as being an ontological view that specifically precludes the intervention of God in the natural world. So, while the multiverse deist may not be able to avail himself of any of the potential benefits of claiming the veridicality of miracles to point toward the existence of God, he will also not be susceptible to any of the objections that the acceptance of miracles carries with it. Given the difficulty of proving that a miracle has actually occurred, I think that the trade-off of denying miracles in return for not having to deal with any of the objections that come with them is beneficial for the multiverse deist and ultimately puts multiverse deism in a stronger position than classical theism.

For the first argument discussed, which raises the difficulty of balancing the need for proof that a particular action breaking one or more particular laws of nature has occurred and that the very same law or laws of nature never have and can never be broken, it is evident how this could prove to be a daunting task for the traditional theist to overcome. Any deistic account, however, while in some respects may be concerned with proving the strength of the latter, will absolutely never find a need or desire to argue for the strength of the former. It is simply not an available consideration, within any deistic account, that any external supernatural force plays any active role whatsoever within the natural world. So, for the deist, it is not a viable explanation, for any event, to say that God made it happen by breaking or suspending some particular law or laws of nature. In the case of a so-called "miraculous event" the deist would likely argue that rather than any kind of natural laws being broken, there is simply a misunderstanding of one or more aspects of what *really* happened. That is to say, rather than a metaphysical issue it would be an epistemic issue. The deist would argue that perhaps we are unclear of certain relevant details or aspects of the event in question, or that we do not have a clear and complete understanding of the relevant natural laws and how exactly they operate.

A similar type of response holds for the second atheistic argument discussed. While Hume's argument does not explicitly rule out the possibility of miraculous events happening, it calls into question whether or not we can justifiably believe that such events have actually occurred, and whether or not we should base any of our beliefs on these allegedly miraculous events. Of course, for the classical theist, there is a lot that comes not just from the occurrence of the miracle itself but also from being able to reasonably believe that the miraculous event occurred and also in the ability to provide believable testimony of that miraculous event. But for the deist, these questions, again, pose no problems because of the demand of causal closure that deism entails. With Hume's argument, we are to proportion our belief to the evidence, and Hume argues that our evidence that natural laws are never broken is far stronger than any evidence that we have that states otherwise, therefore we ought to disbelieve any event that appears to have broken any natural laws. In the event of an alleged miracle the deist, along with Hume, would argue that there are a wide variety of aspects that need to be examined before a particular event can be deemed a miracle, and that if these aspects are scrutinized to the extent to which they ought to be, there will ultimately be a naturalistic explanation for each and every event, be it extraordinary or not. Some of these aspects will include things such as examining the particular law or laws of nature in question and determining whether they are, in fact, laws. It will need to be determined whether or not these laws in question are actually the relevant laws of nature that should have been operational in that particular event. We will have to determine whether or not there was something faulty in the perception of the witnesses of the event, whether or not the initial starting points of various aspects of the event were truly as they were reported or perceived as being, and so on. If we are unable to find a sufficient naturalistic explanation for the entirety of the event in question, then the deist would deem the problem to be an epistemic one rather than a metaphysical one, arguing that there ought to be some naturalistic explanation that is simply epistemically unavailable to us. We would not need to appeal to some external deity to explain an event that we cannot explain; we would simply acknowledge our own epistemic limitations and attribute the event to some unknown naturalistic laws or a misinterpretation of the current laws or of the perception of the event in question.

Finally, the objection that brings forth the apparent inconsistencies between various religions claiming to have miracles that point to the truth of the respective religions to which they correspond would pose no real threat to the deist since the deist would argue that none of these miracles points to the truth of any particular religion. None of these reported miracles are actually miracles. They are simply extremely rare and misunderstood naturalistic events, so none of them can be taken as legitimately revealing any theistic truth. Because of this, there are no inconsistencies or contradictions with regard to miracles within deism as I have described it because, quite simply, deism denies the possibility of any miracles or supernatural revelations within the natural world. On the other hand, to get around this argument for atheism, not only would the classical theist have to demonstrate that the miracles pertaining to his particular religion are veridical but he would also have to clearly demonstrate what it is that differentiates miracles pertaining to his religion from those that pertain to other religions. So the dilemma that this argument for atheism poses for the classical theist is that he must somehow show that only a certain kind of miracles ought to be believed and that all other kinds are to be disbelieved. This would seem to be a challenging task for the classical theist to accomplish, for if he does not, he is still faced with the potential problem of miracles of varying religions contradicting with one another.

CONCLUSION AND PRESCRIPTION

As is evident through the discussion above the deistic response to many of the atheistic arguments aimed at classical theism are very similar, if not the same. Since all of the atheistic arguments discussed above poke at problems that classical theism must address surrounding some aspect or another of God's action in the world, they do not directly harm multiverse deism since deism precludes any such actions. Additionally, the multiverse deist has another route to get around many of these atheistic arguments, by appealing to multiverse responses. The ability to appeal to responses both from the deistic standpoint and from the multiverse standpoint provides the multiverse deist with a great variety of potential replies to different arguments for atheism. The kinds of answers that come from a multiverse deistic standpoint are simply conversation-stoppers, in that once they are issued there really is not much that is left to be said on either side of the argument since, in a very narrow and specific sense, none of these atheistic arguments applies to multiverse deism. Such general and simple answers do little to further any discussion on the matter or to advance any knowledge on the subject. What is needed, rather than a generic multiverse deistic account that simply supplies the same generic response to any atheistic argument is one that provides a certain level of detail and complexity. An account which specifies in what sense God can remain Himself with all of the divine attributes that He is traditionally said to possess while still being causally disconnected from the natural world, and one that specifies the exact make-up and composition of the multiverse.

Details need to be given with regard to how and if any of the divine attributes are maintained or sacrificed within any particular deistic view, and how this relates to the maintenance or denial of the other divine attributes in light of various arguments for atheism, and whether or not this has any bearing on His status as God. Through answering some of these questions many, if not all, of the indirect arguments against deism that have arisen from atheistic arguments against classical theism discussed above, can be addressed and ultimately dismissed. Only when a specified version of multiverse deism is presented, in which these kinds of details are discussed, can we move from deistic responses to atheistic arguments acting as conversation-stoppers, toward detailed multiverse deistic responses that begin to act as conversation starters for further inquiry and dialogue.

NOTES

1. Save for the few specific interpretations of some of the divine attributes that were discussed in chapter 4.
2. Of course, the most well-known version of the design argument is William Paley's discussion of the watch and the watchmaker, which appears in Paley (1848).
3. The most well-known version of the cosmological argument is William Lane Craig's Kalam Cosmological Argument that appears in Craig (1979). More discussion on the cosmological argument can also be found in Rowe (1975).
4. Harrelson (2009) provides a historical account of various versions of the Ontological Argument. While it focuses primarily on arguments from the seventeenth, eighteenth, and nineteenth centuries, it highlights the subtle differences present between arguments in the same family. A similar type of historical discussion can also be found in Barnes (1972).
5. Nowacki (2007) provides substantial discussion on Craig's Kalam Cosmological Argument.
6. Epistemic deism is an alternative kind of deism that is discussed in chapter 6. It argues that God is able to act in the natural world but only at the subatomic level, in areas that are fundamentally beyond our epistemic limits.
7. For example, perhaps God imparted self-sustenance qualities in all entities of the universe, thus requiring no need for His existence to be manifest to us in any way. Or, perhaps, that such a manifestation of His existence is simply superfluous and unnecessary for the overall operation of the world.
8. The differentiation here is between moral and natural evil, where moral evil comes as a result of exercising free will, and natural evil does not.
9. Arguments from evil need not necessarily argue for the nonexistence of God; rather, they can also take the more modest version and argue that the existence of evil renders the existence of God *probably* untrue, as seen in Rowe (2006, p. 80).
10. Ahern (1971, p. 2) further differentiates between, what he calls, the general problem of evil, the specific abstract problem of evil, and the specific concrete

problem of evil. The former two seem loosely to relate to logical arguments for the problem of evil, while the latter is more in-line with the evidential argument for the problem of evil.

11. Some key readings of the logical problem of evil include Almeida (2012) and Mackie (1978).

12. Rowe (1979, p. 337) describes fictional, yet conceivable, idea of a fawn being trapped and horribly burned in a lightning-caused forest fire. After days of laying in agony, burned and trapped in this forest fire, the only thing that finally relieves the fawn of its pain and fear is death. Rowe takes this situation to exemplify a case of gratuitous evil from which no greater good could possibly come.

13. Some key readings on the evidential problem of evil include Rowe (1979, 1996, 2006) and Howard-Snyder (1996).

14. The sense in which "miracle" is being used here is to be defined as a non-repeatable violation of a law of nature.

15. If we also accept that this natural law was broken or suspended by God.

16. Hume's argument concerns itself primarily only with the testimony regarding the occurrence of miracles, but it can easily be expanded to include first-person experiences of miracles as well.

Chapter 6

Possible Alternative Version of Deism

Up to this point, I have discussed and argued for the possibility and plausibility of a certain kind of deism that results from the adoption of a particular type of multiverse model. While I have discussed varying accounts of multiverse models and varying interpretations of specific divine attributes, this has been mainly done to show the range of compatibility between the brand of deism that I ultimately argue for and a broad range of other theological considerations. Since the vast majority of the discussion has been aimed at showing just what viewpoints are consistent and compatible with the kind of multiverse deism that I argue for, this chapter will present a family of accounts called "noninterventionist special divine action" (which I call epistemic deism) that represent an alternative to the kind of multiverse deism that I propose. One detail that I will make clear at the beginning of this chapter is that I have not yet come across any noninterventionist special divine action theories that make any specific mention to the possibility of a multiverse or discuss how such a theory would operate given the existence of a multiverse. For that reason, the forthcoming discussion is limited in the sense that little to no references will be made to a multiverse even though my overall position argues for a multiverse deism. Despite there being no direct discussion of application to or operation within a multiverse, we can extend the discussion below that refers to a single universe to range over any and all universes that exist within a multiverse in the same ways that the kind of deism that I argue for does. This is possible because it is not clear that such an extension is incompatible with any of the noninterventionist special divine action theories in their original form.

I ultimately go on to argue that epistemic deism, while it may be an available alternative, is one that is far more complex and carries with it a substantial amount of difficulties that make it a less-favorable ontological viewpoint than the multiverse deism that I present. As will be discussed below, epistemic deism requires a large number of qualifications, all of which need further explanation in themselves, and the sheer amount of qualifications and "exceptions to the rule" ultimately make epistemic deistic theories far more difficult for one to accept (if they can even be considered as acceptable) than other potential deistic accounts.

Before beginning this discussion it is essential that I point out, however, that none of the noninterventionist special divine action theories that I discuss below are explicitly deistic in any sense, instead that it is only my claim that they can be construed as deistic in nature. The reason that I am discussing these views, in addition to how I think these views can be interpreted as forms of deism, is twofold. The first reason is that noninterventionist special divine action theories may act as motivators for the development of other views of deism. That is, they may open up windows into forms of deism that vary from deism in the traditional sense, allowing us to investigate the true nature of deism further. And, the second reason for the discussion of this kind of theory is that the noninterventionist special divine action theories that will be discussed below are comparably different from classical theism as is the kind of deism that I ultimately argue for. Because of this, they serve as alternative approaches to theism while still maintaining many of the traditional ideas of God, which is similar to what I have set out to do in this overall project.

NONINTERVENTIONIST SPECIAL DIVINE ACTION AS EPISTEMIC DEISM

While there are, of course, a number of possible theistic alternatives to the kind of deism that I argue for, one position that has recently emerged is called "noninterventionist special divine action" (Monton, 2012, p. 134). Though the specific views that fall within this position will vary, the overall position posits that

> [o]ne way for God to [act in the world without intervening] is by acting at the indeterministic quantum level. For example, if there's some quantum process that has a 10% chance of yielding outcome A, and a 90% chance of yielding outcome B, God can, in a particular instance of this process, decide which outcome will result, without violating any laws. (Monton, 2012, p. 134)

That is to say, there are particular aspects of nature, typically at the subatomic level, that are not subject to deterministic laws of nature. These areas, where laws of nature are either nonexistent or indeterministic, are places where God's intervention can fit in with minimal or no obstruction to the overall theories of physics that guide the rest of the natural processes. I interpret such views to be loosely related to the type of deism that we have discussed thus far, but in a way that is distinctly different. For that reason, and for reasons of clarity, I will refer to the deistic position that I have argued for, in which God has no interaction with the natural world post-creation, as "metaphysical deism" while I will refer to this alternative possibility as "epistemic deism" and use this term interchangeably with "noninterventionist special divine action." There are two reasons for this change in terminology. The first is that noninterventionist special divine action generally tends to maintain the appearance of traditional or *metaphysical* deism,[1] *for all we know*, even though that is only because of our epistemic limitations. Thus, given our epistemic limitations, noninterventionist special divine action appears deistic in nature. That is, it is an account of divine causation that relies mainly on our epistemic limitations, and I think that this reliance should be reflected in the terminology. The second reason is that there seems to be some incompatibility between the terms "noninterventionist" and "action" as they appear in the original name of the account. It is not clear in my mind how the two can plausibly coexist since to act seems to entail intervention, whereas I do not think that the same problem persists in the term "epistemic deism." The traditional account of metaphysical deism, as we have seen, is one in which God does not intervene in natural events, thus precluding any sort of miracles or divine intervention. This view generally argues that the universe along with everything material and immaterial within it was created by God in the beginning, but that God then went on a permanent vacation, leaving the universe to operate without His intervention.

There is an expanding literature of different positions of epistemic deism, but I have chosen to focus my discussion on three papers that I think are representative of the kinds of ideas that are pervasive within the overall view. Nancey Murphy, Thomas Tracy, and Bradley Monton develop similar yet distinct accounts of epistemic deism that allow God to intervene in the world without breaking any natural laws. These accounts argue that it is possible, and in some cases necessary, for God to intervene in the natural world through subatomic processes, but that because these interventions occur at the subatomic level, God is able to act without breaking any natural laws. Following from the premises that God acts without breaking any natural laws by keeping His actions at the subatomic level and that miracles are violations of laws of nature, no miracles have occurred, and the integrity of the deistic model is maintained.

Murphy and Tracy both seem to subscribe to differing views of epistemic deism. In discussing the general viewpoint of Murphy, Robert Larmer writes "[t]he indeterminacy that characterizes quantum processes has seemed to some thinkers to suggest a way whereby God can be conceived as acting in creation without abandoning belief in the causal closure of the physical" (Larmer, 2009, p. 550). That is to say, because of the seemingly unpredictable nature of subatomic particles and quantum processes, Murphy thinks that it is possible, or perhaps even necessary, that God is intervening in order to facilitate these processes, but that since there are no deterministic laws of nature that govern the processes at the subatomic level, God's intervention cannot be said to be defying these laws of nature, meaning that the processes facilitated by His intervention cannot be considered to be miraculous, thus maintaining the causal closure of the physical and preserving the deistic viewpoint.

Tracy, on the other hand, argues that because of the indeterministic nature of quantum processes, there are multiple equally possible outcomes that can result from any particular quantum starting point. Because of this, God is able to act at the quantum level in order to realize whichever of these possible outcomes He desires without His actions being deemed as "miraculous" or tampering with the causal structure of nature because each outcome was equally realizable, so God's doing is simply ensuring that one particular possible outcome (that may have arisen anyway) is realized over a variety of other equally possible outcomes.

And thirdly, Bradley Monton presents a version of noninterventionist special divine action in which God can localize "hits" on particular parts of subatomic particles which, in turn, alters the overall makeup of the particle by changing its mass, density, energy concentration, or some other key aspect of it. In making such a change, the overall composition and/or position of the particle have now altered, allowing it to change to a different substance or to move to a different location. That is to say; God can "hit" the particle in such a way that He can effectively change it from a particle of substance A to a particle of substance B, and move it from location A to location B if He so desires. Monton thinks that if these hits can happen in great volume and quickness, then it allows for God to bring about almost any state of affairs without having to intervene in the world.

In this chapter I will discuss Murphy's account of God's interventions at subatomic levels, and provide several reasons why I find her view to be inadequate and ultimately unsuccessful, barring extensive revision and substantial explanation supplemented by an advancement in scientific knowledge of the causal relations between subatomic processes and processes that we see at the macro level. I will then go on to discuss Tracy's account of God acting on the subatomic level, and show how it falls prey to many of the same faults as Murphy's view. Thirdly, I will provide a more detailed account of Monton's view and discuss how, while I find it to be a more complete view than the ones presented by Murphy and Tracy, it still leaves far too many questions unanswered in order for it to be considered a plausible account of God's activity (or lack thereof) in the natural world. Finally, I will go on to discuss how all three of these views fail to address many of the fundamental distinctions required to create an adequate deistic account of God and highlight some of the problems that any account of epistemic deism will face.

NANCEY MURPHY'S VIEWS

Nancey Murphy's paper aims to "provide an alternative account of causation and divine action that is both theologically adequate (consistent with Christian doctrine and adequate Christian experience), and consistent with contemporary science" (Murphy, 1995, p. 326). The position that she ultimately puts forth is that

> In addition to creation and sustenance, God has two modes of action within the created order: one at the quantum level (or whatever turns out to be the most basic level of reality) and the other through human intelligence and action. The apparently random events at the quantum level all involve (but are not exhausted by) specific, intentional act of God. God's action at this level is limited by two factors. First, God respects the integrity of the entities with which he cooperates—there are some things that God can do with an electron, for instance, and many other things that he cannot (e.g., make it have the rest-mass of a proton or a positive charge). Second, within the broader range of effects allowed by God's action in and through sub-atomic entities, God restricts his action in order to produce a world that *for all we can tell* is orderly and law-like in its operation. (Murphy, 1995, p. 339)

That is to say, Murphy puts forth a bottom-up account of causation, divine action, and determinism, arguing that God acts in events at the subatomic level which in turn affects the events at the macro level. Because of the apparent randomness of most subatomic events, argues Murphy, we are left with two options to explain them. Either they are entirely random, or they are determined by God. Because of the principle of sufficient reason, we ought to reject the idea that the processes and events are random, thus leaving only the option that they are determined by God (Murphy, 1995, p. 341). In this sense, since there are no natural laws in operation at the subatomic level, God is able to act at that level, which ultimately influences or determines events at the macro level, without the events being deemed miraculous, thus maintaining the deistic ideal of causal closure as well as the scientific perspectives of causation and natural laws at higher levels.

THOMAS TRACY'S VIEWS

Tracy, much like Murphy, focuses in on subatomic processes, and the explanatory gaps that surround them, as a likely place where God may choose to act. What Tracy means by "explanatory gaps" are cases in which we must admit that we do not have viable and adequate explanations to questions raised by scientific inquiry, or when particular theories entail that we will not in principle be able to give sufficient explanations for some events that are within the scope of that theory (Tracy, 1995, p. 290). Tracy is not in favor of "God of the gaps" kinds of theories, arguing that God is not to be found in what we *don't* know, rather He is to be found in what we *do* know. In most "God of the gaps" theories, the progress of science entails a push-back on the defined role of God in the world, which Tracy feels is not an adequate account of God and His actions. While this may be the case, Tracy believes that there are still some aspects of nature that will, in principle, never be knowable by human minds or scientific advancements, thus allowing a spot to insert God as a causal agent without the risk of having the progression of science force Him out of that position. Of quantum processes, Tracy claims that some

> are so extraordinarily sensitive to their initial conditions that arbitrarily close starting points for these processes can produce dramatically divergent outcomes. The results will be unpredictable in principle, since it will not be epistemically possible either (a) to specify the initial conditions with full accuracy or (b) to predict their result by considering the operation of the system under similar, yet slightly different, initial conditions. (Tracy, 1995, p. 312)

Tracy notes that in many cases trying to provide an account of divine intervention, concessions will often have to be made either on the scientific side or on the theological side to accommodate for the other, but he goes on to argue that if it is the case that the unpredictability of indeterministic chance at the quantum level and the chaotic unpredictability in the system that conveys the quantum effect are both confirmed "then it is open to us to propose that one way in which God may act in history is by determining at least some events at the quantum level" (Tracy, 1995, p. 318). That is not to say, however, that God determines the outcome of each and every quantum event, or that He randomly chooses what outcome will result from each subatomic process, "[r]ather, God will realize only one of the several potentials in the quantum system, which is defined as a probability distribution" (Tracy, 1995, p. 318). In other words, the initial starting point of the quantum process is one that is open to multiple equally possible and equally realizable outcomes, and the intervening role that God plays, on Tracy's account, is that He determines which of these equally realizable outcomes is actually realized in this particular case.

The critical aspects in which Tracy's view differs from Murphy's is that, for Tracy, only *some* quantum processes and events are intervened in by God whereas for Murphy, at least on the surface, it seems as if God's action is required in order for any quantum process to be carried out. Secondly, while it seems that, on Murphy's account, that God has absolute power in determining what the outcomes of each quantum process will be, the same does not seem to be the case on Tracy's view. For Tracy, God's ability is limited to a finite (and perhaps small) number of potentialities that He is able to realize for each respective quantum process.

BRADLEY MONTON'S VIEWS

The main goal that Monton sets out to accomplish in his paper "God Acts in the Quantum World" (2012) is to argue that despite the nature of noninterventionist special divine action theories confining God's active ability to the subatomic world, this does not mean that what God can accomplish through His actions is limited in any sense. Monton aims to show that, even by acting only on subatomic particles, God is still able to accomplish great things such as parting the Red Sea or turning water into wine (Monton, 2012, p. 133).

Monton's overall account relies on the GRW theory, which he describes as follows:

> [T]he GRW theory [named after its proponents, Ghirardi, Rimini, and Weber] is an indeterministic version of quantum mechanics that allows for indeterministic "GRW hits" to happen on the wave function of a particle, thus localizing the wave function. This means that a majority of the mass density of the particle is in a small region of space, but the wave function has tails that go to infinity, so the mass of the particle is also spread out throughout this infinite region of space. The GRW hit can happen anywhere that the wave function is non-zero, so the GRW hit can happen anywhere in space, concentrating most of the mass density for the particle in that region where the GRW hit happened. (Monton, 2012, p. 137)

Given Monton's acceptance of the indeterministic nature of subatomic processes, God's activity can be inserted into this level without the risk of violating any particular laws of nature. Because of the nature of the indeterminacy of the GRW theory, Monton goes on to argue that, for those who want to maintain the existence of an active God,

[w]ithin the constraints of the laws of the GRW theory, God can make a GRW hit happen anywhere, on any particle, or collection of particles. This gives God the power to move particles around, anywhere in the universe. And moreover, God can do so arbitrarily quickly, just by making the GRW hits happen in an arbitrarily small amount of time. (Monton, 2012, p. 137)

So unlike Murphy and Tracy, Monton does not argue that it is necessary that God intervenes in order to facilitate all or some subatomic processes. Instead, he only aims to show that God acting in a particular way at the subatomic level is compatible with the GRW theory, of which he is a proponent. Monton has also attempted to provide an account of how God's actions at the subatomic level can lead to grand outcomes at the macro level, ultimately making God's active abilities quite expansive.

EVALUATION

While Murphy's view has several attractive points, namely that it (a) maintains physics as it is, at both the macro and the micro levels, (b) eliminates the supernatural at the macro level, (c) preserves the causal closure of the physical at the macro level, (d) excludes irregularities like miracles, and (e) still allows for the existence and intervention of God, it has received its share of criticism, specifically with regards to the scientific aspects of how quantum processes actually work, in that processes in the micro world rarely relate to events in the macro world. If this is the case, it raises the ever-present question, in anything relating to God's intervention in the natural order of things, of what the reasoning behind God's alleged intervention would be. Of course, the response that we can never truly hope to imagine God's reasoning behind any action He commits will always be present, but it still stands to make the case that it would be peculiar for God to choose to intervene in the natural order of the world in order to facilitate the actualization of some subatomic quantum processes that have no translation into anything in the macro world. That is to say, to actualize some subatomic process that has no influence whatsoever on anything at all. To do so would simply seem to be pointless and a waste of time. It just seems as if it would be out of God's nature to be continually intervening in (arguably) meaningless subatomic processes that have no effect on the natural world. In this sense, Murphy needs to do more work in demonstrating, scientifically, the causal connections between events at the micro level and events at the macro level.

Of course, the previous objection can be argued on several grounds (as noted above), but even in the case that that objection is refuted, it still remains that God's intervention in the world, be it at a subatomic level or not, is an intervention nonetheless, which is fundamentally contrary to the view proposed by metaphysical deism.[2] The key component to Murphy's argument that allows it to subscribe to a deistic model while at the same time argue that God is active within the world is that deism precludes miracles, miracles are violations of laws of nature (at the hand of God), there are no laws of nature in place with regard to subatomic processes, therefore God can intervene in subatomic processes without breaking any laws of nature (since none exist at the relevant time and place), thus maintaining a deistic model that is consistent with God's intervention in the natural world. So, in a sense, by arguing against the fact that any natural laws are being broken by the intervention of God, it is as if Murphy is arguing for a view that is not quite metaphysical deism, but also not quite epistemic deism. She seems to be arguing for a very narrow kind of metaphysical deism in which causal closure is demanded, but in which the definition of causal closure is an odd one, where it simply means that no natural law has been broken.

Somewhat related to the objection above is Murphy's claim that God acts on and affects macro-level events by acting on micro-level events, creating a bottom-up causal connection. Murphy argues that there is a scientifically proven connection between micro- and macro-level events, while Larmer argues that it is scientifically proven that there is no such connection. Given this lack of clarity, regardless of whatever the actual case may be, we are left with two options: either (1) there are no causal connections between micro- and macro-level events, or (2) there are causal connections between micro- and macro-level events. If the first case is accurate, and there are ultimately no meaningful causal connections between micro-level and macro-level events (which is a view that Murphy would object to), then there would be no reason to think that the principle of sufficient reason should apply to micro-level events solely because it applies to events at the macro level (which is, itself, arguable). If this is the case, then this would leave open the option for the chaos theory of quantum processes, meaning that the apparent randomness of quantum processes is just that, random. This raises a secondary question of whether or not "randomness" should be considered a sufficient reason under the principle of sufficient reason, because while it seems that Murphy would say that it should not be, others may argue that it should be, and if the latter is even a possibility then this would mean that Murphy has stricken a completely viable option that is consistent with the principle of sufficient reason, a principle that she argues so heavily for. Lastly, as mentioned earlier, a disconnect between micro-level and macro-level events would also mean that any actions performed by God at this level would be utterly pointless (at least to us) since they would in no way influence anything taking place at the macro level. Again, this is not the view that Murphy would take, but I am simply presenting it to show what the consequences would be for Murphy's view should it turn out that, scientifically, such a causal connection did not exist.

On the other hand, if there does exist a causal connection between micro-level events and macro-level events, as Murphy argues, since macro-level events display law-like behavior, it seems hard to believe that such law-like behavior would simply stop upon reaching the micro-level. There is simply no reason provided that would lead us to believe that everything in the universe would display law-like behaviors and then suddenly cease to maintain such behaviors at a certain point, and this is something that Murphy needs to explain in order for her account to stand up as a plausible theistic account. It would seem more likely that perhaps the behaviors that these subatomic particles are displaying are cohering to some natural laws but, for whatever reason, we are simply not able to discover or understand them. The fact that we have not yet discovered or come to understand these potential laws does not mean that they are not in operation. If it is the case that there are some sort of natural laws governing subatomic processes, then it would mean that there is no need to invoke the presence and intervention of God to explain their causation, and Murphy's account would fail. Even if we set that aside, however, and God does intervene in order to facilitate or actualize subatomic processes, it is not entirely clear how Murphy's view is so different from the classical conception of God, save for the fact that He is in a sense limited to *only* acting at the subatomic level. This seems like something that proponents of the classical conception of God would be opposed to since it, at least on the surface, constrains God's ability, and something that proponents of metaphysical deism would oppose because it prescribes God's intervention in the natural world. So, in both cases, whether there are causal connections between micro-level events and macro-level events, or not, we can see how Murphy's account could be rejected in the first case, or require serious revision in the second case.

Finally, it seems to me that in this case, Murphy is working with a distorted definition of traditional deism, what I call metaphysical deism, in which her view is only deistic at the macro level. While it is true that metaphysical deism would preclude miracles, it does not just preclude miracles; rather, it precludes any sort of intervention whatsoever. It demands causal closure, and whether or not there are any natural laws at play is simply irrelevant to whether or not any kind of external or divine intervention is permitted under metaphysical deism. Whether a particular external intervention happens to find some loophole in which no natural laws are operational, thus preventing it from being declared a miracle is not of concern here. The main concern is whether or not an external intervention defies the causal closure of the natural world that is proposed by metaphysical deism and it seems that any external intervention, miraculous or not, would defy that causal closure thus making any view that supports both divine intervention and metaphysical deism inconsistent. Any such view must ultimately be dismissed. On the same note, it seems that a scientific account of the world would demand causal closure as well, which would pose a significant problem for Murphy's overall project of trying to create an alternative account of divine intervention that maintains both theological and scientific integrity. The traditional Judeo-Christian conception of God is one in which He, while perhaps intervenes in the universe, does not *reside* in it. That is to say, while He impacts it, He is not a part of it, which seems entirely contrary to the causal closure of the atheistic model generally put forth by modern science. These two claims simply do not seem to be able to coexist, at least on this account. What Murphy has done is presented a theologically inadequate view of Christian doctrine, as well as an inadequate view of science in order to create just enough of a gap to fit in a theory that attempts to satisfy both sides of the equation.

Overall, Murphy's view appears to be an attempt at finding a way of incorporating divine intervention into metaphysical deism. Murphy would argue, as far as I can tell, that metaphysical deism demands a causal closure of the universe, but she proposes a view in which specific divine actions are permitted since they would not count as breaking the causal closure of the universe. Thus, allowing for a version of metaphysical deism in which God can freely intervene in the universe at the micro level. I think that Murphy's attempt fails in this respect because allowing for any kind of divine intervention within a metaphysical deistic theory is simply contradictory, and therefore I have tried to look at her view as proposing a version of epistemic deism, which seems like it could be more in line with some of the claims that she makes. If, however, this view is to be interpreted as an account of epistemic deism then, there are a variety of questions that I mention in the opening chapters that must be addressed and answered before Murphy's account can be taken as a complete worldview.

Tracy's view, while much like Murphy's, is far closer to what I have described as epistemic deism and is subject to several problems as well. The first problem that arises, which seems to be one that is almost inherent in these sorts of theories, is that the introduction of God into any explanatory account of nature means that the system on which He is acting cannot be causally closed and that any intervention within that system would be epistemically problematic. That is to say that

> [t]he idea of a direct act of God is unacceptable for us because such an event would involve a gap in the order of nature; it could not be sufficiently explained in terms of antecedent finite events, and so would constitute "an absolute beginning point" for a novel causal series . . . such an event is not epistemically problematic, it is "literally inconceivable," for the notion of an event without

"adequate finite causes" is "quite as self-contradictory as the notion of a square-circle." We must, therefore, rigorously avoid all talk of divine action *in* history. Nonetheless, it is open to us to think of history as a whole as God's act. (Tracy, 1995, p. 301)

So, the problem that Tracy's theory faces is precisely one that he describes at the outset of his paper. Of course, while it is not entirely clear whether or not this is the case, it could be that Tracy views his theory as one in which history as a whole is an act of God, in which case it would be plausible to think that his view is left untouched by the "absolute beginning point" objection. Tracy's view, however, even if it is one that views all of history as a whole as an act of God, still maintains that God makes continuous interventions in the world through His manipulation of quantum processes. Despite the fact that God would only be actualizing one of the several equally realizable effects of any given quantum starting point, the need for a cause that originates within the system itself still remains, otherwise the "absolute beginning point" objection stands. There would still be a series of quantum processes and effects that cannot be adequately explained by one or more finite causes within the closed system. So, much like Murphy, Tracy seems to argue for a view in which the macro level is causally closed while the micro level is causally open.

A second problem that Tracy's view faces is that he needs to figure out how to properly deal with the apparent limitations on God's power in his conception of how and when God acts in the world. A difference between Tracy's view and Murphy's view is that in Murphy's view God seems to have near complete freedom in what effects to actualize for each particular quantum starting point, whereas in Tracy's view He does not enjoy that luxury. For Tracy, God can only actualize one of a limited number of equally realizable potentialities that are already associated with each quantum starting point. It is not entirely clear whether or not this is so because God is limited to these options by something other than Himself, or if He *chooses* only to avail Himself of one of these options (and this is something that Tracy needs to clarify), but if it is the case that God is limited in His abilities of which outcome to actualize then this would indicate a limitation on His powers, which is something that many theists would most likely object to, since it would deny God some sort of creative power. This being the case, Tracy needs to do some explanatory work to describe (a) his conception of what omnipotence entails, and (b) how this conception can be maintained despite the apparent limitations on God's causal power when it comes to actualizing particular outcomes for various quantum starting points.

A final area where Tracy's view needs further explanation is the discussion of what quantum processes God chooses or is required, to act on. Tracy's theory proposes, unlike Murphy's, that God only acts to determine the outcome of *some* quantum processes, not all. It is not altogether clear why it is the case that God only intervenes in determining the outcomes of some quantum processes, and not all, or none. Let us suppose that there is a 50/50 split between the micro-processes that God intervenes in and the micro-processes that are allowed to run their natural course according to the natural laws that are in place. Tracy needs to explain why exactly it is the case that God does not simply intervene in the outcomes of *all* quantum processes, as in Murphy's view, since it would seemingly be no extra "effort" for God to make that move and increase His activity in the determination or influence of quantum process outcomes from 50 percent to 100 percent. On the other hand, Tracy also does not make it entirely clear why God's intervention is required in any quantum processes at all. If we are to go back to the original 50/50 split, with 50 percent of all quantum processes being left untouched (directly) by God and left solely to operate under the natural laws that are in play, then there needs to be an explanation about what makes the other half of quantum process outcomes so special as require or call for God's intervention. Even if it is the case that God has some particular will that can only be realized through the specific outcome of a particular micro-process then it would seem that, given God's omnipotence and omniscience, He could have foreknown each particular situation and set up the natural laws in such a way as to generate the desired outcomes of each and every quantum process so as to realize any and every desired outcome that He may have. Furthermore, He could have done this without being forced to intervene in the natural order of the world directly. With that in mind, it seems almost arbitrary to decide which events are those that were influenced by the hand of God, and which ones were purely the results of the operational natural laws, and Tracy provides no explanation of how such a distinction is to be recognized.

Moving on to Monton's account, I think that he provides a far more complete account than either Murphy or Tracy do, in that it is both more detailed while also more conservative in its aims. While both Murphy and Tracy argue that it is necessary that God acts at the subatomic level to actualize some or all subatomic processes, Monton makes no such claim. He simply aims to show that God's action at the subatomic level is compatible with GRW theory and that despite God's action being limited to the subatomic level the outcomes that arise from it are not as limited as one may think.

Despite some of the strengths of Monton's argument, it is still not altogether clear what would motivate God to act in such a system. While this may not have been a specific question that Monton aims to explicate in his paper, it is still a question that remains. It seems as if, with the natural laws already in existence within the GRW theory, there is simply no need to invoke the activity, or even the existence of God. Granted, this theory can be viewed with the caveat that it is intended for those who want to maintain the existence of God, but unlike the views of Murphy and Tracy where God's action seems necessary to facilitate particular subatomic processes, the same cannot be said for Monton's account. So one thing that Monton needs to explain is why his view needs an active God, or even a God, at all.

Another aspect in which Monton's account could benefit from further explanation is that, while he provides a substantial explanation of how God's action at the subatomic level translates into visible outcomes at the macro level, he says nothing about why God's actions need to be limited to the subatomic level. Other than the fact that it seems to be a prerequisite of noninterventionist special divine action theory nothing is said about either why God's active ability is confined to the micro level or why He chooses to keep His actions to the micro level. So again, it seems that the only motivation for having an account that relegates God's active ability to this level is for reasons related to making them undetectable by us, which is the prime component of epistemic deism. So while Monton's GRW account makes substantial improvements on the views of Murphy and Tracy by (1) providing a substantial explanation of the theory of physics with which he aims to demonstrate the compatibility of God's actions, (2) clearly demonstrating how God's actions at the micro level translate into meaningful events at the macro level, and (3) being far less ambitious in his overall argument by trying to show only that God's action at the subatomic level is compatible with rather than required by a particular account of physics, there are still questions that remain to be answered.

THOUGHTS ABOUT THE OVERALL RELATION TO EPISTEMIC DEISM

Through the discussion of all three views that have been put forth by Murphy, Tracy and Monton we have seen that they are each in line with aspects of epistemic deism, in that they all generally argue for God's intervention in the universe, but that these interventions can and do only happen at levels and in ways that are epistemically inaccessible to us. The discussion has also gone to show a variety of problems that are present within these types of theories, namely that there is an enormous amount of explanation that must go into each and every detail within the theory. The reason for that is because any theory that can be reduced to a version of epistemic deism is essentially a theory that is based on justifying varying numbers and degrees of exceptions within itself—namely, how God can intervene in a causally closed system.

The term deism typically connotes, among other things the causal closure of a system, but epistemic deistic theories try to posit and justify ways in which divine intervention can be permitted yet maintain aspects of that causal closure. In the case of epistemic deism theories, the claim is often that divine interaction occurs at levels that are unknowable to us, therefore leaving the world (as far as we can and will ever know) as causally closed. This simply does not seem right since it would entail that God's actions would be limited by and dependent on the intellect of humans, in that, He only chooses to do actions that we cannot know about. With our knowledge of science and physics constantly advancing this would seem to result in God's active abilities becoming more and more limited as our knowledge progresses and there is something that seems fundamentally wrong about that inverse relation. Furthermore, it seems that we could also say that epistemic deism makes God's intervention substantially undermined, if not altogether pointless in one sense since, on it, we would never know how or when God is acting on or in the natural world. This lack of knowledge of when and how God is acting seems to undermine at least one of the points of divine intervention, which is the knowledge that the intervention is coming from God. Of course, these are just some possible objections to the overall account of epistemic deism, and the epistemic deist could respond by arguing that there is some sort of upper threshold to the limits of human knowledge, but it still goes to show that all epistemic deists face an uphill battle in trying to justify how they aim to maintain a deistic undertone in their theories that is based on the human capacities for knowledge while at the same time allowing God to act but still placing limitations on His acting abilities. Furthermore, causal closure is something that either does or does not obtain, regardless of whether or not there is some conscious knowledge of it. It seems that epistemic deists are arguing that our ignorance of the fact that there is no causal closure in the natural world entails that there is causal closure in the natural world, which does not seem right. It simply does not appear that the epistemic deist will ever be able to wholly and satisfactorily create a substantial account of how and why certain limitations are able to be placed on God, and how or why specific actions that He does do not count against the requirement for causal closure of the universe that any theory labeled as deistic should entail.

Furthermore, the epistemic deist will need to answer the question of what exactly makes his theory deistic in any sense. Again, since deism generally tends to entail causal closure, which is an aspect that epistemic deistic theories lack, it is not entirely clear just how these theories can be appropriately labeled as deistic. To take it one step further, the epistemic deist will also need to answer the question of how his view ought to be distinguished from classical theism. While it appears that the interventions that God makes in the world under the epistemic deism framework would generally tend to be very subtle and, by definition, unknowable to us, it is not clear that this kind of action would be inconsistent with a version of classical theism. Some versions of classical theism could, in theory, argue that God is active only in ways that are unseen by us, so the epistemic deist would have to provide some amount of explanation to differentiate his view from such a version of classical theism.

Finally, as alluded to earlier, for any account of epistemic deism, there is a need to describe what kinds of limitations are placed on God and His activity within the universe. The common thread, as noted, that will be present is the epistemic boundary of God's actions. The epistemic deist will have to detail exactly what kinds of limitations, if they are to be more complex than the simple "unknowability" of them, are placed on God and His creative ability since epistemic deism entails limitations on God's creative ability be it in scope or method. The epistemic deist will also have to detail why exactly these particular limitations are relevant and necessary for his particular account, as well as detail how these limitations are able to coexist with the absolute nature of most of the divine attributes.

With all of the problems mentioned above, both specific to Murphy's, Tracy's, and Monton's views, and those addressed to epistemic deism in general, and it is almost as if each claim made within an epistemic deistic theory simply raises more questions than it answers. Of course, each individual theory may be able to deal with some, or even most of these problems, but I am not convinced that any version of epistemic deism will be able to adequately address all of the questions raised. Each adequate answer to one question will simply result in pushing off some contradiction, counter-intuitive thought, or highly debated claim to the end of the line, where eventually it will show itself to weaken, if not destroy, the plausibility of the account.

CONCLUSION

Here we have discussed the views of Murphy, Tracy, and Monton as three views that represent noninterventionist special divine action. I have discussed how these views, both individually and collectively, can be construed as deistic in nature, but in ways that are markedly different from deism in the traditional sense, as well as in the multiverse sense that I propose. I have argued that neither of these three views nor noninterventionist special divine action theory as a whole is a satisfactory theistic[3] ontological view in that there are substantial difficulties that they each must overcome. Ultimately, the view rely on a series of justifying exceptions so as to allow for God to act in certain ways within the world, and no reasonable justification has been shown or hinted at to allow these exceptions, essentially rendering each view to be a skewed version of traditional (metaphysical) deism or otherwise a skewed version of classical theism.

The examination of these views, despite their overall implausibility, allows us to investigate them in comparison to both deism and classical theism, raising questions into the exact nature of each and allowing us to further explore how much room there is for movement within each respective view. If we are to reject these noninterventionist special divine action theories based on them being incompatible with classical theism or deism, then the classical theist and deist must, respectively, solidify the conceptions of their views, demonstrating and explaining how noninterventionist special divine action theories do not fit within their larger ontological views.

NOTES

1. While both *metaphysical* deism and *epistemic* deism are both metaphysical ontological views, *metaphysical* deism is an ontological view that is concerned only with the metaphysical, whereas *epistemic* deism concerns itself both with the metaphysical and with the epistemic.

2. Again, none of the discussed authors explicitly subscribe to deism; rather, I make the claim that their views can be construed as deistic.

3. Theistic only in the sense that they posit the existence of God.

Chapter 7

Potential Difficulties and Further Lines of Inquiry for the Multiverse Deist

Up to this point, I have provided an account that details how the acceptance of a multiverse theory that posits the existence of all possible realities entails a deistic God (if we are to maintain the idea that God exists) rather than the God of classical Judeo-Christian monotheism. I have argued for the plausibility and potential advantages of multiverse deism but have primarily done so with little to no mention of any of the potential pitfalls that the multiverse deist may have to overcome to make a case for the plausibility of his view. To leave the discussion without the mention of any possible disadvantages or hurdles that still must be overcome would be to provide an incomplete analysis and paint an unrealistic picture of multiverse deism. To be sure, there are additional potential drawbacks and points of debate to be faced by multiverse deism, as there are with any theistic viewpoint, to the few that I will mention here. The remaining potential difficulties that I will present are ones that I think are most pressing for the proponent of the multiverse deism, and the critical challenges that someone ought to strongly consider in determining whether or not they think such a view is plausible and ultimately worthy of adoption. Notably, the potential difficulties that will be discussed can also serve as a starting point for further research and inquiry within the topic. I do not think that any one of these difficulties that will be presented is particularly devastating to the overall account of multiverse deism, instead I have deemed that each one of these problems is essentially beyond the scope of this particular project and think that a brief acknowledgement of them, as well as a call for further inquiry into them, is sufficient for the present purposes. There are two main reasons why each of these potential problems is beyond the essential nature of this project. The first is that, because of the broad sense in which I have described the kind of multiverse deism that I argue for there are a significant number of replies that can be offered to each potential difficulty, all of which are dependent on the particular conceptions of God or the multiverse that are being assumed. That is, a multiverse in which each universe comes to pass in some sort of cyclical model of big bangs and big crunches will yield a different response to some objections than will a multiverse in which each universe coexists simultaneously with all others. Similarly, various interpretations of God's necessity, or position relative to time, will yield different responses to specific objections. Secondly, the objections to be discussed are, in many cases, linked to broader and more significant issues than those explicitly contained within the objection itself. It is not as if these objections can be dismissed rather easily or with a quick note of clarification; instead, some will require substantial explanation and elucidation of the nature of God and/or the multiverse in order to provide a full-fledged response. To cover each potential response and to adequately treat the broader implications to which each of these objections is linked is simply not a practical undertaking in a project such as this, and so will have to be dealt with on a case-by-case basis given the specifics of each particular viewpoint.

Each one of the forthcoming sections in this chapter could be likely be expanded to cover a full paper, chapter, or even research project, but to leave a philosophical discussion about the nature of God and the universe without any unanswered questions, while a worthy endeavor, is likely unachievable. It is important to remember that, while many of these potential problems are framed in a way as to specifically address proponents of the multiverse, deists, and multiverse deists, they are often not problems faced exclusively by members or those groups. Rather, within the difficulties that will be discussed below are questions that persist within any kind of theological thought, requiring insight from across the disciplines of philosophy and theology, not just left for the multiverse deist to address. Because of the nature of many of these potential difficulties, they will also serve as areas in which further lines of thought can be explored. Each of these difficulties generally tends to call for more in-depth discussion and detail on a particular aspect concerning multiverse deism and, as such, while potentially being seen as an objection can also be seen as an opportunity to provide a response that allows for more profound elaboration on particular aspects of multiverse deism. The overall result of this further discussion will be a more substantial understanding of both multiverse deism and the nature of the particular objection to which it is responding.

Several difficulties for the theist in accepting a multiverse theory alone have been discussed in chapter 3, but these difficulties will be revisited here.[1] Moving through the subsequent sections there will be discussions on difficulties that may arise for the multiverse deist from explaining a deistic God's role in creation of the universe, the need to determine the location of a deistic God within the multiverse, the need to abandon the idea of a personal relationship with God as the greatest possible good, reconciling the idea of a non-active God with the biblical accounts of an active God and, finally, accounting for the various miracles and religious experiences that have been reported throughout history.

REVISITING DIFFICULTIES FOR THE THEIST IN ACCEPTING A GENERAL MULTIVERSE THEORY

As was discussed in chapter 3, the theist already faces several difficulties just in the acceptance of a general multiverse theory, and these difficulties arise even before any of the added potential problems of accepting a deistic multiverse theory are introduced. Since this chapter is devoted to the difficulties that will be faced through the acceptance of the overall account of multiverse deism, I feel it is a good idea to quickly revisit some of the ideas and difficulties that were previously discussed in chapter 3.

The first issue that was discussed dealt with the amounts or kinds of individual universes that populate the multiverse. The strongest theistic multiverse view, as I see it, is one that is not only theologically and logically consistent, but one that is also supported by a certain degree of scientific evidence. That is to say, for a multiverse theory to contain no logical inconsistencies and to be theologically compatible, while it may confer possibility, is not enough to confer plausibility on any particular multiverse model. Some level of scientific evidence for the physical viability of such an account is required in order to supply, or raise, a level of overall possibility for any given multiverse account.[2] The potential problem for the theist arises in that the scientific accounts of the multiverse often call for a large number of universes, generally including universes that the theist may not want to accept as being metaphysically possible.

Scientific accounts of the multiverse generally concern themselves only with the physical possibility of the existence of specific individual universes when determining whether or not they ought to be included as part of the multiverse. Science considers only things such as physical constants in determining the overall possibility of a universe, leaving out other considerations such as moral value, overall happiness, presence of sentient life, and so on. These latter considerations, the ones typically ignored by scientific approaches to the multiverse, can often play substantial and even foundational roles in theistic accounts of the multiverse. That is to say, where the physicist will set his threshold for inclusion in the multiverse at a location that represents only physical possibility of existence, the theist will set his threshold at a place that considers not only physical possibility of existence but one that also reflects various ethical considerations, various life-form considerations, or a whole host of other theological considerations that would be required by their faith to confer worthiness and plausibility of existence on any given universe. The consequence of that is that the scientific case for the multiverse will almost always call for a multiverse that is populated with more universes than any theistic case, and this is simply because of the varying conceptions of what entails "possible" when evaluating the existence of possible universes.[3] What this means is that if the theist hopes to strengthen his position on the existence of a multiverse by appealing to scientific evidence then he is likely to have to make some concessions to the theological aspect of his account, since there will be some tension between the scientific side and the theological side in deeming what universes can be included as members of the multiverse. So one thing that the proponent of the philosophical multiverse needs to determine is, if he has hopes of maintaining any threshold below which a universe's existence is not possible, not only whether his particular account is compatible with a scientific account of the multiverse but also more generally of whether any philosophical multiverse account that posits a value-based threshold is compatible with any scientific multiverse account.

The second potential issue raised is that the acceptance of a multiverse theory by a theist undercuts, if not altogether completely denies, design arguments (Megill, 2011, p. 133). Design arguments are typically aimed at, through any number of ways, making the case that our universe is ordered in such a way as to prove that it is the product of intelligent design.[4] The arguments aim to deny the idea that the universe could have simply come to be the way that it is out of chance or simply as the result of unguided natural processes. Since design arguments are typically predicated on highlighting the uniqueness of our universe, when taken in conjunction with a multiverse account, the overall strength of the argument seems to diminish. This difficulty is one that is expressed by Roger White in his writing:

> [Many] who write on the subject suppose that M[ultiverse] and D[esign] are more or less on par; both can solve the puzzle of life's existence, so our preference for one over the other must be based on other grounds. If what I have argued is correct, this is a mistake. While both hypotheses, if known to be true, would render life's existence and indeed my existence unsurprising, only the design hypothesis is confirmed by the evidence. The multiple-universe hypothesis may indeed undermine the argument for design, but only to the extent that we have independent reasons to believe it. (2003, p. 247)

What is important to note about White's words, aside from him opting in favor of design arguments over multiverse theories, is his claim that the two do not seem to be able to co-exist, at least not in their strongest forms, stating explicitly that the multiverse undermines design arguments.[5]

The multiverse deist has several options here. To get around the problem of the potentially undercut design argument, the multiverse deist either will have to discount the overall need for the design argument in arguing for his case, by appealing more heavily to other kinds of arguments both for the existence of God and for the existence of the multiverse, or else needs to show how the multiverse is compatible with design arguments. The first approach, if the multiverse deist chooses to take it, would be to convey the message that the loss of strength in the design argument is minimal to his overall case because it was never a critical factor in arguing for the existence of a deistic multiverse in the first place. To lose a small piece of argumentative ammunition is no big problem, in that there may remain multiple other, stronger, pillars on which the overall deistic multiverse account is built. The second approach that can be taken by the multiverse deist is to reframe the design argument in such a way as to support the existence of a multiverse. By arguing that the complexity of a multiverse far exceeds the complexity of a single universe, the multiverse deist may be able to claim that the existence of a multiverse points more to an intelligent designer than does the existence of a single universe. Rodney Holder, who is firmly against the evidence for the existence of a multiverse even acknowledges, if at least minimally, that "there is . . . the logical possibility that God designed and created infinitely many universes" (2006, p. 57).

Many multiverse accounts argue for a multiverse that is comprised of all possible universes. While the idea of just what "possible" entails may vary from multiverse account to multiverse account, we can typically say that this would entail a vast number of universes.[6] Given the number of universes within the multiverse, making our universe just one of several or one of many possible universes, it would seem to be the case that the existence of our universe was simply inevitable. Regardless of the construct of the multiverse, be it one that ranges infinitely into time, one that ranges infinitely into space, or both, the existence of each and every possible universe, including ours, is guaranteed to occur at either some time or some place within the multiverse. If that is the case, then it appears that any evidence of intelligent design that is displayed in our universe is merely the result of chance being actualized, rather than of a specific, intentional plan of God. This leaves the theist with several options if he hopes to continue on a pursuit of arguing for theism. On the one hand, he can proceed to make his argument for theism with the diminished strength of the design argument, appealing more heavily, or exclusively, to other arguments for God's existence. On the other hand, he can proceed with his argument for a theistic multiverse and try to amend or re-conceptualize the design argument in such a way so that it also applies to a multiverse with a comparable level of strength that it enjoys when applied to a single universe.

The final issue mentioned is one surrounding ethics and morality within a multiverse, which is a problem also faced by modal realists, as addressed by Robert Adams (1979) and Yujin Nagasawa (2015). This is a potential problem for theists who aim to adopt a multiverse model that both allows for individual counterparts to exist in different universes within the multiverse and also posits that every possible state of affairs is or will be realized within the multiverse. That is to say, this is a potential problem for advocates of multiverses that posit that a particular individual can exist in universe U^1, have a counterpart who exists in different universe U^2, still another counterpart in universe U^3, and so on throughout the rest of the universes in the multiverse in which each possible outcome will be realized. The problem that arises is that if there is a multiverse populated with a significant number of individuals and their counterparts, then the level of individual responsibility and accountability to "do the morally right thing" given certain situations is decreased because of the idea that elsewhere within the multiverse their counterpart will do what is morally right. Yujin Nagasawa summarizes the problem faced by modal realists and, in turn, multiverse deists in saying,

> The problem for modal realism is that the view appears to discourage us from acting morally because whether or not we act morally and prevent evil in this [universe] evil is instantiated in some other possible [universes] anyway. This is because, given the claim of modal realism that all possible [universes] exist, the total sum of good and evil does not change whether or not we act morally in this [universe]. (2015, p. 187)

The problem discussed by Nagasawa, while directed at modal realism, can clearly be applied to multiverse deism as well, or any multiverse account, for that matter.

If it is the case that every possible outcome shall arise within the multiverse then whether or not I choose to do a good act in this particular universe is trivial, from a moral perspective, since my refusal to do said good act will simply make it necessary that one of my counterparts in another universe actualize that good act. Similarly, if I do carry out that good act, then it will prevent that act from being actualized in the same situation by my counterpart elsewhere in the multiverse. Since it is not clear that the same good deed enjoys any more moral worth in one universe than another, the personal responsibility of making morally right choices seems to be diminished, if not altogether lost.

This problem is not insurmountable, as we have seen a reply from David Lewis (1986, p. 127),[7] rather the multiverse proponent will just have to formulate, in addition to a standard view of morality and ethics, a way in which his view of ethics can be applied to a multiverse in such a way as to account for triviality as a result of the existence of potential or actual counterparts.

One way of going about this, for example, may be to make an argument for the value of indexical considerations in moral and ethical judgments. That is to say, as Lewis would argue, whether or not a doing a morally praiseworthy act will be actualized elsewhere in the multiverse, it is still best if this action is carried out in this particular universe. Of course, there are a number of considerations that need to be taken into account in such a claim, but the basic idea remains that it is better to have a good act occur here and now than in some other universe at some other time. So, the multiverse proponent would have to adopt or generate a view on morality that either accounts for such issues or otherwise explain why he does not think that that is an issue for his account of the multiverse.

GOD'S INACTIVITY DESPITE HAVING ACTED ONCE

We can now move on to discuss some issues that will be faced by the multiverse deist in particular. The first potential problem, from this standpoint, to be discussed is the problem of explaining why it is the case that God acted only once in creation and then subsequently refrained from and continues to refrain from undertaking any subsequent actions. Whether we see a divine inactivity because God does not know that He needs to act, He does not have the ability to act, He does not have the desire to act or because He does not have the need to act there still seems to be, at least on the surface, a level of incompatibility between an ontological view that argues for non-active God but that also argues for a God who created the multiverse. That is to say, the multiverse deist needs to ask what it is that makes it acceptable for one to believe that God acted in one very particular and specific case, while simultaneously holding the belief that it is unacceptable to posit that God acts at any other time subsequent to that initial act.

One who discusses the establishment of and explains a similar distinction is Niels Gregersen (2008). Kile Jones (2010) summarizes Gregersen's position in saying

> that the distinction between *special* divine action (SDA) and *general* divine action (GDA) cannot be maintained. SDA is the idea of an action committed by God that brings about specific and unique physical consequences. GDA is closer to . . . the fall-back position—history as a whole as a single act of God. Gregersen thinks this distinction cannot be maintained because "*any* divine action must be treated as both special and yet as falling within the over-all pattern of divine self-consistency." (Jones, 2010, pp. 582–83)

The kind of distinction that Gregersen and Jones discuss is slightly different than the way that I have framed the distinction that needs to be made by the multiverse deist, but the general idea remains: that there needs to be a distinction made between different types of divine action. So while, Gregersen discusses a distinction between what he calls special divine action and general divine action (2008, p. 179), the way that I have set the difficulty out is that there needs to be a distinction between two different examples of special divine action. Whether the former or the latter kind of distinction is more difficult to make, I am unsure,[8] but it is a problem that must be solved nonetheless.

Of course, the problem of explaining creation and the activity of God (or lack thereof) is not exclusive to multiverse deism; instead, it is a problem that all theistic viewpoints must face. Because of this, it is not altogether clear that explaining the process of creation is one that is unique to multiverse deism, or that it is even a problem at all. The difficulty for the deist arises in explaining what differentiates this particular act from any other kind of acts that God could potentially carry out. While many theists will not take it as a point of debate, rather as a brute fact, that God created all that exists out of nothing, I am not wholly satisfied with this answer provided by theism and so the multiverse deist, as well as any other kinds of theists, ought to do a bit more explanatory work in describing the various potential methods by which God came to create all that exists. The classical theist, assuming that he ascribes to a view arguing that God created the universe(s) *ex nihilo* faces the task of explaining just what that means and how it is possible. Similarly, the multiverse deist will likely have to make the same explanations but, in addition to this, he will then have to go on to explain why this single act of creation by God (if it is deemed an act) can be accepted under a worldview that is based so heavily on the idea of a God who does not act on the natural world. So, while providing an explanation for creation is not solely a problem for multiverse deists, there is an added level in which the multiverse deist must explain what it is about the specific initial act that makes it different from any other subsequent divine acts; the kinds that it precludes.

So, the task of the multiverse deist is one that is markedly different and more difficult than the classical theist. In addition to providing an account of how the multiverse was created (presumably *ex nihilo*) the multiverse deist must also (a) come up with an explanation for why God's initial act of creation cannot truly be deemed an act, (b) come up with an explanation for why God's initial act of creation was not an act on the natural world, or (c) come up with an explanation for why God's initial act of creation was an act on the natural world but is permissible in, or does not contradict, an ontological view that precludes God acting on the natural world. The common thread that can be found in each of these three options is that the multiverse deist must provide an account of how the initial divine act of creation is to be distinguished from any other kinds of subsequent divine acts in such a way as to allow it to be consistent with the overall deistic viewpoint while still maintaining that any other subsequent divine acts are inconsistent with the viewpoint.

DETERMINING THE LOCATION OF GOD

The task of determining where exactly God is to be placed within a deistic multiverse theory is a difficult one with a variety of different possibilities. Of course, the kinds of possibilities that are available will vary depending on the particular kind of multiverse to which the multiverse deist ascribes, but for our purposes here we will keep with the multiverse that entails a large number of spatiotemporally isolated universes that collectively exhaust all possible realities. Even in taking for granted that God is a necessary being, the overall problem can be reduced to a question about how exactly we are to interpret God's necessity. Whether God can be located in time or at a specific location is a question that any theistic account will have to deal with, but the insertion of a multiverse theory simply adds one more level of complexity to this already tricky topic. Paul Sheehy (2006) worries about this precise problem as it relates to modal realism. Of a realist, multiuniverse theory that posits the existence of counterparts, Sheehy says, "God is not reductively analyzable into entities present in [universes] or the relations in which they stand. Talk of God as a necessary being thus eludes elucidation in the realist framework of modality" (2006, p. 318). He goes on to say that

> [e]ven if we accept that a unique individual possessed of great-making properties exists at every possible [universe], a radical revision of the classical conception is required. For, now there is a single God for each [universe]. Is the object of worship in the actual [universe] our God alone? Or is it the mereological sum or set of Gods? The former view seems to violate too much the sense in which God is unique and the latter undercuts any clear sense in which God is unitary. (Sheehy, 2006, p. 319)

While Sheehy's discussion is aimed explicitly at modal realism, his concerns still apply to multiverse deists, and he has raised several key issues that must be addressed. And as he has framed it, with only two options available, neither of these two options is particularly attractive for the theist in that they each require substantial undesirable concessions be made about the overall nature of God.

The distinction between whether or not God necessarily exists for the multiverse or whether or not God necessarily exists for each universe is something that will have to be considered by the multiverse deist. If God only necessarily exists for the multiverse, then there is the possibility of having a significant number of universes in which God does not exist. It may be difficult for some theists to accept a notion like that, not wanting to concede the possibility that this universe is one in which God does not reside. Similarly, if God necessarily exists for each universe, then the multiverse deist will have to detail exactly how it is possible that God exists (presumably simultaneously) in a number of spatiotemporally disconnected universes. For this, explanations will have to be given as to the sense in which God exists within each universe. For example, whether He is in one location within the universe, whether His existence permeates the entire universe, whether He is part of the universe or whether the universe is part of Him, and so on. Crafting such an explanation is no easy task, for this is an aspect of the discussion of God that will cut across a wide range of other considerations such as the interpretations of God's eternality, timelessness, essential nature, and so on. So to decide on a particular conception on how to locate God is quite complex and can shape, or be shaped by, other attributes of God in very significant ways.

A further consideration is that, if God is not located within or among any or all of the universes in the multiverse, then an account will have to be provided of where there is space for Him to reside either within or outside of the multiverse. That is to say, the multiverse is thought to be composed of only universes so there would, theoretically, be no space between any of these universes for God to situate Himself. The totality of the multiverse is exhausted by the universes of which it is comprised, so it is not clear how anything can exist outside of a universe yet still remain in the multiverse. If there is such a space, then the multiverse deist would have to provide an account of just what this mysterious space between these many universes is, and what differentiates this space from the space that we would find within the bounds of a typical universe. Similarly, if God is to be placed outside of the multiverse, essentially looking in from outside, since the multiverse is thought to contain all that exists, the multiverse deist will have to explain how it is possible that anything (even God) can exist outside of the multiverse. This would seem to require that God be either spatially or temporally distinct from some or all of the multiverse. And if it is the case that God can reside on the other side of the multiverse limits there needs to be an explanation of why this does not leave open the possibility for other beings, things or entities to also reside on the other side of the multiverse boundary. In this case, however, the multiverse deist will again have to find a way of explaining and reconciling the fact that many of the universes within the multiverse do not, in the simplest sense, contain God. One potential way of getting around this problem is to construct some explanation as to how God's presence, even though He may be centrally located elsewhere, essentially permeates all points of the multiverse. Or perhaps some sort of formulation akin to pantheism could help to defer the problem. This would allow the multiverse theory to maintain at least some sense of God's existence within each universe, even though it may seem to be a reduced sense of existence, one that the deist may not be enthusiastic about accepting.

This task of locating God, for the multiverse deist, is no small task. As we have seen, there are a variety of considerations and factors that ought to be considered, both practically and theologically, if he hopes of providing a satisfactory account of where God is located in relation to the multiverse. Ross Cameron (2009) offers a reply to the worries about the location of God, put forth by Sheehy (2006) by arguing that God can be conceived of as a universal, putting Him at a level comparable to numbers, which would allow Him to be present completely in every location but confined to no specific location at all times. Whether such an account is reasonable is another question, but it does show that there are some potential avenues that can be taken by the multiverse deist in the hopes of addressing the problem of locating God.

ABANDONING THE IDEA THAT A PERSONAL RELATIONSHIP WITH GOD IS THE GREATEST POSSIBLE GOOD

One of the things that both theists and atheists alike have done their best to maintain is the idea that a personal relationship with God is the greatest possible good.[9] Religious theists often use this claim to call for increased levels of worship from their followers, proposing that one will not receive or be part of a personal relationship with God if they do not devote themselves entirely to that particular faith. You must, in essence, put yourself in the proper position to experience the greatest possible good, and such a position can only be entered into via faith, prayer, church attendance, and so on. The reward for all of this sacrifice and devotion is a potential taste of that greatest possible good—a personal relationship with God. Many theists would, and do, find this trade-off well worth it.[10] Atheists, on the other hand, argue that if it is the case that the greatest possible good is a personal relationship with God, then we should expect to see far more people enjoying that relationship. That is to say, an omnibenevolent God would want the best for all of His creations, and we clearly see many people who want and strive to achieve a personal relationship with God, making what seem to be the requisite sacrifices and putting themselves in the proper position to experience Him, but that personal relationship never comes. The atheist would claim that surely there cannot exist an omnibenevolent God who would fail to provide so many of His creations from the greatest possible good. Therefore, argues the atheist, since we see a lack of personal relationships with God, He, as we conceive of Him, does not exist.

The multiverse deist, or any deist (for that matter), will not only have to abandon the idea that a personal relationship with God (in the most basic sense) is the greatest possible good, but also have to abandon the idea that a personal relationship with God is a good at all. Since the possibility of having a personal relationship with God would seem to entail some sort of reciprocity between the subject and God, such reciprocity would entail God acting in the world in some sense, which is clearly something that is precluded by multiverse deism. For an ontological view to place such a high value, or any level of positive value at all, on something that it precludes merely does not seem plausible. For that reason, the multiverse deist, in denying the possibility of a personal relationship with God must also deny the idea that such a relationship carries with it any sort of positive value as well. There is no doubt that this comes as a massive compromise for a significant number of theists, and it is a compromise that many will, presumably, not want to make. So this is potentially the biggest hurdle for the multiverse deist to overcome since this is likely the place where most theists will make the decision not to get on board with multiverse deism, even if they find it plausible in other areas.

Why the abandonment of this idea is such a potential problem for the multiverse deist is because the high value of a personal relationship with God is one that has been held so firmly by many theists for centuries, and is still a key idea in Western religion today. Many people throughout history who have purported to have enjoyed a personal relationship by God have often been viewed and treated as god-like in their own right, often going on to be greatly celebrated and admired both by the church and by its followers.[11] Of course, that is not to say that all those who claim to have had a personal relationship with God have gone on to live celebrated celebrity status, but the fact remains that those who enjoy such relationships, and have these relationships confirmed or approved by the church or their peers, are often thought more highly of. That is because, regardless of the actions or character of the individual, the value of the good of a personal relationship is so high that he who is fortunate enough to enjoy such a good is often elevated in status. The foundation of many faiths is based on one or more individuals being touched, in one way or another, by God and going on to spread His message to followers. So to deny the good of such a relationship is essentially to deny the foundation of many religions.

The denial of a personal relationship with God as being a good which, in turn, brings into question the foundation of many different faiths, poses a problem for the acceptability of multiverse deism for theists who already ascribe to a particular faith that fits that mold. As was discussed at the outset of chapter 4, one of the attractive points of the conception of God that I propose is that His attributes do not vary substantially from the attributes of the God of classical theism thus making the possibility of shifting from belief in classical multiverse theism to multiverse deism an easy one, in theory. This problem, however, is the roadblock in making that smooth transition from classical theism to multiverse deism. Because of that, the multiverse deist will need to find some way of creating a pathway to allow for many classical theists to abandon or reconsider the cherished idea that a personal relationship with God, if there is any hope of gaining mass acceptance based on a transition from another theist viewpoint.

A middle-ground, so to speak, in reconciling this difficulty may be in the reframing of the conceptualization of what exactly it means to have a personal relationship with God. That is to say, maybe there is some hope for the multiverse deist in crafting a conception of a personal relationship that does not entail reciprocity from God toward us. Multiverse deism does not explicitly preclude a personal relationship with God, rather it precludes a reciprocal relationship with God, and there is a chance that that distinction is enough space for the multiverse deist to maintain the long-held idea that a personal relationship with God is inherently good. If he is able to do that, while it may not be as satisfactory a conception as some classical theists would like, it would undoubtedly be favored by them to the outright denial that such a relationship is possible or holds any good whatsoever. Similarly, the multiverse deist may be able to hold some ground by maintaining that a relationship with God is the greatest possible good while still denying the realization of it, but then going on to provide an account of how the two sides can co-exist.

ABANDONING THE LITERAL INTERPRETATION OF THE BIBLE

Very closely related to the abandonment of the belief that a personal relationship with God is the greatest possible good is the abandonment of the literal interpretation of the Bible, or any religious scripture, in cases that call for direct divine intervention. Of course, religious scriptures are often essential and serve as a foundational for their respective religions, so to demand that certain aspects of these scriptures be interpreted in a particular way or even ignored altogether is no small request.

While it is undoubtedly the case that some theists take the accounts of God's intervention in the world, as depicted in scripture, to serve merely as analogies or stories that do not truly make claims about God's interaction with the world, there still do remain a significant number of people who interpret those scriptural accounts literally. For some, to make the claim that certain aspects of scripture ought not to be taken as veridical is to make the claim that all scripture is not to be taken as veridical,[12] and so to expect wholesale acceptance of the abandonment of literal interpretation of scripture is a very lofty ambition. The common reason for wanting to deny such a request, I would imagine, would be something along the lines of making the claim that the removal or ignorance of those particular sections of scripture would have severe and negative ramifications across the entire faith. That is to say, those cases of divine intervention that are described in scripture are essential to the faith itself, and to ignore, remove or devalue them is to alter other aspects of the religion as well, things such as ethics and morality, the nature of God, and so forth.

Thomas Jefferson, an American deist, undertook the task of removing nearly all mention of miracles and divine intervention from the New Testament in the early nineteenth century. In constructing his book "The Life and Morals of Jesus of Nazareth," often referred to as the Jefferson Bible, Jefferson (2007) used a razor and glue to cut and paste together sections of the New Testament. The result was, essentially, a condensed version of the New Testament that was devoid of all mention of miracles by Jesus Christ, any supernatural activity, and any mention of Jesus Christ as divine. To undertake such a task as merely removing any kind of supernatural discussion from scripture is not very difficult, as we see, it can be done simply with a piece of scripture, a razor and some glue. But the real question that remains is whether or not the new, altered version of the scripture, such as Jefferson's Bible, carries with it a drastically different meaning or proposes different values than the original scripture. It is not altogether clear what Jefferson's intention was, in constructing the Jefferson Bible, but one could imagine that his goal was to create a document that still maintained the core prescriptions, doctrines, values, and ideals of Christianity without having to appeal to instances of divine intervention or miracles. To demonstrate that we need not hold on to all of these accounts of alleged divine interaction in order to have a fully functioning religion in which we can still have faith, and that can still guide us to live our lives morally.[13] Of course, whether or not this was Jefferson's true intention is unknown, and if it was, whether or not he was successful in achieving his goal is open to interpretation. With that in mind, this is precisely the task that the multiverse deist will have to undertake if he hopes to be successful in persuading followers from classical theism. He must ultimately construct, or defend, an idea similar to the one proposed by Thomas Jefferson, and show how such an idea is at least on par with the original scripture.

Of course, it is not clear that a significant number of people adopt a literal interpretation of the Bible or any scripture, for that matter, so this may not be as big of a problem for the multiverse deist as initially thought. But even with that being the case, this is not a potential problem that multiverse deist can simply dismiss. While it may not be the case that a significant number of people wholly interpret scripture literally, with many people taking particular sections to represent analogies, life-lessons, and so on, they may interpret other aspects in a literal sense. So, while the number of people who interpret the Bible completely literally may be minimal, the number of people who interpret the sections relevant to the proponent of the deistic multiverse (sections involving divine intervention or revelation) literally may be far greater, and that is where the potential problem arises for the multiverse deist. William Bristow writes that "a deist typically rejects the divinity of Christ, as repugnant to reason; the deist typically demotes the figure of Jesus from agent of miraculous redemption to extraordinary moral teacher" (Bristow, 2010). Given the deistic outlook on the status of Christ, he is tasked with trying to persuade others to accept that, and other similar claims.

The different ways in which people interpret the same scripture has always been a topic of debate within theology and the church, but more importantly for the multiverse deist will be exploring ways in which a single individual may come to interpret different parts of the same piece of scripture in competing ways. That is to say, one thing that may need to be investigated is the way in which, and the reasoning behind why an individual may interpret specific sections of a particular piece of scripture literally, while he will interpret different sections of that same piece of scripture as metaphors or analogies. While this may seem to be more of a psychological study than a philosophical one, information on this line of thought would be valuable for the multiverse deists (in addition to other philosophical views) in order to help determine how to go about bridging the gap between belief in multiverse deism and belief in classical theism, and how one may be able to move from one to the other.

ACCOUNTING FOR THE MIRACLES THAT HAVE BEEN REPORTED THROUGHOUT HISTORY

Depending on how one looks at it, it may or may not seem outlandish to see a good number of people admit that they do not believe that miracles or religious experiences actually happen in today's world. Given the level and accessibility of modern science, it seems that more and more people are inclined to accept that, even though they may not have knowledge of what the particular explanation is, there is some sort of naturalistic and scientific explanation for many or all of the unusual or unexplainable occurrences that they may come to witness or experience. While it may be the case that people are increasingly attributing present-day events to naturalistic causes, it may be a much more difficult task to get the same amount of people to attribute many alleged miracles and religious experiences of the past to naturalistic causation.

It is not clear exactly how many miracles have been claimed or confirmed by organized religion over time, but it is fair to say that there are a good number of miraculous events on record and that at least several of these alleged miracles serve as cornerstones for the faith itself. While the "church, through time, has become more open and progressive in light of the challenges posed by modernity . . . this is not to say that the change has come easily" (Jones, 2010, p. 575) there is no doubt that organized religion, as a whole, would like to maintain the credibility of as many miracles as possible, be they cornerstones of that particular faith or not. For the multiverse deist, not only does he have to deny that any miracles are currently taking place, but he also has to deny that any miracles have ever taken place, including those that have been confirmed by the church and taken to be pillars on which the faith stands. So while the average person may be able to be persuaded that no miracles are currently taking place, essentially accepting the causal closure of the world, he may be reluctant to accept that no miracles have ever taken place. This is the problem facing the multiverse deist, allowing for the acceptance of his view to range into the past to cover all time periods, not just the present. There just seems to be something different, and more difficult, about retroactively applying today's scientific explanations to past miraculous events. It is simply more challenging to ask that somebody abandon the belief of some of these core events, even if the occurrence of these past events is in direct conflict with their current beliefs. So while we may find an individual who would say it is preposterous to assume that today we can see the resurrection of a man as God's incarnate, this same person may also simultaneously hold the belief that Jesus was the human instantiation of God and that he returned from the dead. And that is the problem that the multiverse deist may have to face, in attempting to gain acceptance—allowing people not only to accept its views in light of present-day happenings but also to accept its views in light of each and every preceding event in history.

One avenue of inquiry into a topic such as this may be to explore the relation between perception and belief as they relate to time. In cases such as the one described above it seems that there is no difference in the kind of event taking place, and the only difference is the perception of the possibility of the event given the different historical times in which each took or will take place. Just because something is historical, does it require less intellectual scrutiny before being accepted as veridical? If so, we need to explore what the other relevant factors are that make one claim of resurrection worthy of belief while another claim of resurrection is not. Once questions like this are answered then perhaps the multiverse deist will be able to move one step closer to full-fledged acceptance of the deistic multiverse view that ranges back through history than just a present-day deistic multiverse view.

CONCLUSION

In this chapter, we have seen some of the issues that will need to be addressed by the multiverse deist if he hopes to forward a complete ontological view. Ranging from reconciling the discrepancies between the kinds of universes that will populate the multiverse on scientific accounts and the kinds of universes that will populate the multiverse on philosophical accounts, the issue of having the design argument undermined, problems with morality and counterparts, differentiating God's initial act of creation from other potential subsequent acts, determining the location of God within the multiverse, conceding that a personal relationship with God cannot be the greatest possible good, calling for the abandonment of the literal interpretation of certain aspects of the Bible to, finally, accounting for all of the miracles and acts of divine intervention that have been reported throughout history. While these issues are certainly not exhaustive of the list of additional considerations that the multiverse deist will have to account for, they are some of the most pressing. Furthermore, I have deemed that none of these issues are fatally damaging to multiverse deism on the whole and that there are a number of ways in which each of them can be replied to. I have simply noted that to forward responses to each of these issues is beyond the scope of this project based on the sheer number of individualized responses that will need to be given according to the specific type of deistic multiverse that is being argued for. Each of these is best dealt with on a case-by-case basis.

NOTES

1. For some additional objections to the multiverse, see Holder (2006).
2. The possibility of which is disputed by Rodney Holder, who states that "[f]or a start, these [other] universes [within the multiverse] are completely unobservable. A theory is only really scientific if it makes predictions about things we can observe and the multiverse fails this test disastrously. The problem is that we cannot even in principle have any contact with the other universes" (2006, p. 56). On this, Holder seems to think that our ability to confer any level of scientific proof to the existence of a multiverse is extremely low if existent at all.
3. Both Kraay (2012, p. 149) and Johnson (2014, p. 452–53) discuss issues related to the vagueness of thresholds for inclusion within a theistic multiverse.
4. For a more detailed discussion and examples of different kinds of design arguments, see Ratzsch (2010).
5. This is a claim that Saward (2013) argues explicitly against, claiming that such a statement, while perhaps correct in some cases, does not apply to all multiverses.
6. Exact numbers are not important here, but the idea is that the number is large enough to discount the uniqueness of our universe.

7. Almeida (2015) also offers a brief reply to the worries of Adams (1979).

8. Jones (2010, p. 583) does not think that the former is a substantial problem that cannot be solved.

9. Or at least an exceptionally highly valued good.

10. The idea of this trade-off was popularized by Blaise Pascal, who argues that it is in one's best interest to believe in the existence of God and to act accordingly, regardless of whether or not we know that God actually exists. This is discussed by Janzen (2011), Jordan (2006), Sobel (1996), Chimenti (1990), Brown (1985), Rescher (1985), Hacking (1972), and Webb (1929).

11. An idea similar to this has been argued by Fales (1996) as a reason to motivate people to falsely claim religious experiences, and this idea has been objected by Gellman (1998) and Harper (2014).

12. Of course, logically, this is not the case. In practice, however, this is a substantial issue.

13. Whether the religion was morally guiding people, to begin with, or not is another question altogether but, for the sake of argument, let's say that it was/is.

Chapter 8

Practical Considerations and Concluding Thoughts

The preceding discussion undertaken in this project has dealt with the argument for, and the pros and cons of, multiverse deism as a viable alternative to classical theism. Much of this discussion focused on philosophical and theological conceptions, logical entailments, and other considerations that do not necessarily make their practical consequences obvious. This chapter addresses some of the practical concerns that arise from the adoption of multiverse deism in favor of classical theism, and discuss how such a reconsidered ontological view can have real-world effects that are not purely confined to the pages of academic papers or to the informal discussions in the hallways of university philosophy and theology departments. The first half of this chapter will address these practical considerations. The second half of this chapter will simply provide some concluding thoughts and offer a summarized view of the ideas and issues presented up to this point.

A SHIFT IN ARGUMENTS FOR ATHEISM

The acceptance of multiverse deism as a plausible alternative to classical theism would not simply mean that there is one additional ontological view to add to the list but with that addition may come some changes in the ways that philosophers of religion think about, and ultimately construct, arguments for atheism. Many of the current arguments for atheism are designed for, and directed against, the traditional conception of God rather than a deistic God or the God of a multiverse. And this is with good reason. The traditional conception of God is just that, *traditional*, so it carries with it the richest history and the most considerable number of proponents. So, there is no question as to why a great many of the arguments for atheism are aimed at bringing into question various aspects of this traditional conception. Where the problem arises is if a plausible alternative to the classical conception of God emerges, one to which the vast majority of existing arguments for atheism are inapplicable. This is where the practical consideration shows itself for the philosophers of religion, particularly those who aim to dispute the existence of God.

As was shown in chapter 5, several of the predominant families of arguments for atheism (divine hiddenness, the problem of evil, problems with miracles) pose significantly less of a threat to multiverse deism than they do to classical theism. The result of this is a two-pronged attack on arguments for atheism as they are currently formulated. On the one hand, if the plausibility of multiverse deism is taken seriously and adopted by a substantial number of people, then the atheists will need to come up with new arguments that specifically address and attack multiverse deism. To be fair, there are substantial arguments for atheism and significant arguments against the existence of a multiverse but none that I know of specifically address multiverse deism. Even though many of these particular arguments do not directly address multiverse deism, some aspects of them may still apply so, in this case those who wish to oppose multiverse deism will need to, minimally, reframe many of the current arguments for atheism or against the multiverse so that they are suitably aimed at and apply to multiverse deism specifically. Of course, expecting the wholesale acceptance of multiverse deism over classical theism is slightly ambitious, so it is not clear that such a drastic measure of reformulating all atheistic or anti-multiverse arguments to be directed at multiverse deism is a task that atheists will have to deal with any time soon, but it is still something that will need to be considered, as multiverse deism could still be a potential reply to an atheistic argument by somebody who aims to maintain the existence of God.

The second prong of the attack on current formulations of arguments from atheism, while not nearly as extreme as the first, is far more likely, still raises a serious practical consideration for atheists and their arguments against the existence of God. Given the resistance of multiverse deism to current arguments for atheism, which we have seen comes largely from the specific interpretation of various divine attributes, the classical theist can potentially import some of these particular interpretations into his own conception of God. What I mean by this is that, even if one does not see the overall idea of multiverse deism as plausible or favorable to classical theism, he can still acknowledge that there are aspects of multiverse deism that are superior to the relevant aspects of classical theism. For example, one may accept that the idea of omnipotence as divine efficiency stands up better to certain arguments for atheism than does another way of interpreting omnipotence within the classical conception of God. So, in a case such as this, while the atheist does not have to concern himself with formulating a whole new atheistic argument directed against multiverse deism, there is still an aspect of multiverse deism that has made its way into, at least this particular interpretation of, omnipotence within classical theism. And it is this interpretation of omnipotence that the atheist will then have to construct a new argument against, rather than any other traditional account of omnipotence to which he would have been previously accustomed.

So, whether or not multiverse deism is accepted in its entirety, there will be some adjustments that will have to be made by the atheist in terms of his arguments against God's existence. In the first case, where multiverse deism is accepted, it is simply an entirely new way of thinking about the existence of and nature of God, so the atheist's arguments will have to be reframed in a way as to attack the plausibility of a different ontological view from which they are accustomed to attacking. In the second case, where multiverse deism is not accepted, it is possible that some aspects of it are imported into classical theism, and though atheists will not have to restructure their arguments to account for an entirely new ontological view, they will have to reframe some of their arguments to account for smaller, specific interpretations of specific aspects of God's nature, such as a particular divine attribute.

RE-EVALUATING WHAT IT MEANS FOR GOD TO BE PRAISEWORTHY

Determining what exactly it means for something or someone to be praiseworthy, even if we limit our discussion to the case of God, is no simple task. Determining whether or not the God of the deistic multiverse, however, is praiseworthy is another discussion altogether, but one that is necessary if we are to consider such an ontological view as plausible. In the case of the God of classical theism, we can say that He is praiseworthy for a variety of reasons; He is able to perform a great deal of tasks; He is greater than us in any and all respects; praise of Him will result in rewards for us later in life or in the afterlife; and so on, but it is not altogether clear that these same things can be said about the God of the deistic multiverse. Depending on the emphasis that is placed on each of these factors that can potentially determine praiseworthiness, it may turn out that the deistic God is not praiseworthy, or perhaps just substantially less praiseworthy than the God of classical theism. For one who takes reward of praise as a critical factor in determining whether or not a deity is praiseworthy may not find any compelling evidence to deem the deistic God as praiseworthy, since His abilities to acknowledge and reward praise are severely limited, if not altogether nonexistent, when compared to the potential rewarding actions that may be granted under a different ontological view. Similarly, if one determines that the deistic God is praiseworthy, then he must also determine in what ways to praise Him, and determine what, if anything, he hopes to achieve through this praise.

So, this discussion, while not limited to the multiverse deist, holds several extra dimensions to be discussed that the classical theist will not have to deal with. But, given the overall complexity of such a discussion, the few additional dimensions that come with a multiverse deistic view should not be seen as a further devastating complication to the idea of divine praiseworthiness.

UNDERSTANDING THE ROLE OF ORGANIZED RELIGION

Somewhat connected to determining what constitutes praiseworthiness is the task of determining the role of organized religion in light of a deistic God. Because, if it turns out to be the case that it is against God's nature to act in the natural world, is there really any theistic purpose for organized religion? That is to say, if the deistic multiverse is as I have described it, then things will (I would imagine) play out the exact same way for us whether we engage ourselves in organized religion, or not. Of course, this presupposes that organized religion carries with it, and is heavily based on, the idea that petitionary prayer and actions can and will be answered by God, and this presupposition may not necessarily be the case. With that in mind, for the multiverse deist, it would seem that organized religion as a vehicle for petitionary prayer would be abandoned. That would then force us to answer the question of whether or not organized religion maintains any value and, if so, what kind of value it maintains and what kind of role it can continue to play in our society.

This question seems to be one that turns into a sociological discussion rather than a philosophical one but is still an important consideration nonetheless. Even for those who subscribe to the traditional conception of God and who attend church regularly, some may already see organized religion not necessarily as a vehicle to foster some sort of reciprocal relationship with God; rather, they take it as a social opportunity. It can be seen as an opportunity to meet other people that you may not otherwise meet, to foster a sense of community with others, to take the time out to reset the priorities of a busy life once a week, or any other practical function that may not be related to God in any way. The simple idea here is that it is not the case that everyone will be forced to abandon all of the goods of organized religion through the acceptance of multiverse deism. Many of these religious benefits can still be maintained, and organized religion can still play an important and positive role in the lives of many people despite the belief that a reciprocal relationship with God cannot be formed. The simple fact is that for many, however, the overall theistic motivations and purpose from which many of these other sociological goods are merely a by-product will have to be substantially reframed.

OVERVIEW OF THE DISCUSSION

The overall argument that I have made in this research project came in the form of a multi-part conditional. I argued that if we accept the existence of a multiverse model that calls for the existence of all possible realities, and that we aim to maintain the idea that God exists, then this entails the existence of a deistic God rather than the God of classical theism. Furthermore, I argued that the existence of a deistic God is preferential to the God of classical theism when it comes to addressing particular arguments for atheism.

I began by presenting an overview of the multiverse discussion, in chapter 2, from both the philosophical and the scientific perspectives. This showed that the multiverse is a serious ontological view being researched by a good number of credible individuals across different disciplines and that it ought to be given substantial consideration as a viable ontological view. It also highlighted the variety of different types of multiverse that are currently being discussed by philosophers and physicists, and I was able to specify that the kind of multiverse model that I was going to be operating with for the remainder of this research project was a multiverse comprised of universes that collectively exhaust all possible realities. While I noted that I specifically did not want to establish any threshold for conference of possible within such a multiverse structure, throughout the remainder of the discussion of this project, it should be clear that such a threshold, minimally, includes the specification that there exists no universe in the multiverse in which God is active.

Moving into chapter 3, I outlined several of the difficulties that the theist will have to face and account for in accepting a multiverse theory that calls for the existence of all possible universes. Some of these difficulties would not be exclusive to theists; rather, they will apply to anyone accepting that brand of multiverse. I addressed the overall thesis of this research project and detailed how the theistic acceptance of a multiverse theory that calls for the existence of all possible universes entails a deistic God rather than the God of classical theism. And finally, in this chapter, I discussed how various accounts of free will and determinism play out in the multiverse in light of a deistic God, showing how various conceptions and combinations of free will and determinism are compatible with the deistic multiverse theory for which I ultimately argued.

Chapter 4 began with a discussion on the vague nature of the deistic God, and some of the potential reasons behind that lack of clarity throughout history. Because of the lack of explicit divine attributes or interpretations of these divine attributes within the historical literature of deism I took the overall conception of the deistic God to be open. This openness allowed me to discuss my interpretations of omnipotence and omnibenevolence of the deistic God. I discussed omniscience, timelessness, immutability, and necessity, as these were some of the divine attributes that did not seem as crucial the overall deistic conception as those discussed in previous sections but still needed to be addressed in a discussion such as this. Finally, the last section of this chapter discussed how each of the particular interpretations of the divine attributes discussed up to that point ultimately factored into the overall conception of the deistic God that I presented.

Chapter 5 was divided into two parts. In the first half of the chapter I discussed the teleological argument, the ontological argument and the cosmological argument in order to show how a deistic conception of God is compatible with these common arguments for the existence of God. In the second half of the chapter I discussed the problem of divine hiddenness, the problem of evil, and problems with miracles as several of the stronger and more well-known contemporary arguments against God's existence that generally pose problems for the classical theistic conception of God. Finally, I discussed how a generic deistic conception of God might be able to get around some of the difficulties that classical theism faces in dealing with these arguments and showing that deism may be able to respond to some of these atheistic arguments adequately.

In chapter 6, I presented a possible alternative to the kind of deism that I propose. This alternative was called noninterventionist special divine action, but I referred to it as epistemic deism. I detailed the nature of three different noninterventionist special divine action theories and discussed why and how they can all be reduced to epistemic deism. I went on to describe how epistemic deism as a whole is an unviable ontological view and is ultimately inferior to the kind of deism that I argued for in this project.

Finally, in chapter 7, I discussed some potential difficulties and further lines of thought that the multiverse deist will need to address at some point, but that are ultimately not within the scope of this project. I began by revisiting several difficulties for the theist in accepting a multiverse theory alone were discussed in chapter 3. Moving through the remainder of the chapter there were discussions on difficulties that may arise for the multiverse deist from explaining a deistic God's role in creation of the universe, the need to determine the location of a deistic God within the multiverse, the need to abandon the idea of a personal relationship with God as the greatest possible good, reconciling the idea of a non-active God with the biblical accounts of an active God and, finally, accounting for the various miracles and religious experiences that have been reported throughout history. The goal of this chapter was simply to mention some of the other lines of research that can be carried out, as a result of the work that I had done to that point.

In conceiving of and completing this project, while I made several arguments for the existence of a deistic God and for some particular interpretations of His nature, the overall goal was to open the discussion on, what I felt was, an under-discussed ontological view. Coming into this project I felt that deism could have been a plausible ontological view with some potential upsides and, in moving through my research, I think that I not only have confirmed that feeling but was also able to point out specifically why it is plausible, where the upsides to deism are and bring to light some areas where it is potentially weak as an overall view. My hope was that, in bringing up this under-discussed topic of deism, and discussing it in relation to the multiverse, which is one of the most active areas in the philosophy of religion today, that I could rekindle some interest in this ontological view as a plausible alternative to classical theism. This work will, hopefully, serve as the starting point for much more research and discussion on deism, either as it relates to the multiverse or as a stand-alone ontological view.

References

Adams, R. (1979) Theories of Actuality. In Loux, M. J. (ed.) *The Possible and the Actual: Readings in the Metaphysics of Modality*. pp. 190–209. Ithaca, NY: Cornell University Press.
Ahern, M. B. (1971) *The Problem of Evil*. London: Routledge & Kegan Paul Ltd.
Almeida, M. (2012) The Logical Problem of Evil Regained. *Midwest Studies in Philosophy* XXXVI. pp. 163–76.
Almeida, M. (2015) The Prosblogion: The Philosophy of Religion Blog. *Is Modal Realism Immoral?* [Online]. Available from: http://prosblogion.ektopos.com/2015/02/05/is-modal-realism-immoral/ [Accessed 6 February 2015].
Aristotle. (1998) *The Nicomachean Ethics*. David Ross (translated). Oxford: Oxford University Press.
Barnes, J. (1972) *The Ontological Argument*. London: The Macmillan Press.
Bristow, W. (2010) Stanford Encyclopedia of Philosophy. *Enlightenment* [Online]. Available from: http://plato.stanford.edu/entries/enlightenment [Accessed 20 December 2015].
Brown, G. (1985) A Defence of Pascal's Wager. *Religious Studies* 20. pp. 465–79.
Buckareff, A., & Nagasawa, Y. (2016) *Alternative Concepts of God: Essays on the Metaphysics of the Divine*. Oxford: Oxford University Press.
Byrne, P. (1989) *Natural Religion of the Nature of Religion: The Legacy of Deism*. London: Routledge.
Cameron, R. P. (2009) God Exists at Every (Modal Realist) World: A Response to Sheehy. *Religious Studies* 45(1). pp. 95–100.
Carr, B. (2007) *Universe or Multiverse?* Cambridge: Cambridge University Press.
Chimenti, F. (1990) Pascal's Wager: A Decision-Theoretic Approach. *Mathematics Magazine* 63(5). pp. 321–25.
Craig, W. L. (1979) *The Kalam Cosmological Argument*. London: The Macmillan Press.
Craig, W. L. (1980) *The Cosmological Argument from Plato to Leibniz*. London: The Macmillan Press.
Deutsch, D. (1997) *The Fabric of Reality*. Harmondsworth: Penguin.

Dougherty, T. (2011) Recent Work on the Problem of Evil. *Analysis Reviews* 7. pp. 560–73.

Dougherty, T., & McBrayer, J. P. (eds.). (2014) *Skeptical Theism: New Essays*. Oxford: Oxford University Press.

Draper, P. (2004) Cosmic Fine-Tuning and Terrestrial Suffering: Parallel Problems for Naturalism and Theism. *American Philosophical Quarterly* 41. pp. 311–21.

Ellis, G. (2011) Does the Multiverse Really Exist? *Scientific American* 305(2). pp. 38–43.

Fales, E. (1996) Scientific Explanation of Mystical Experience, Part 1: The Case of St. Teresa. *Religious Studies* 32(2). pp. 143–63.

Forrest, P. (1996) *God Without the Supernatural*. Ithaca, NY: Cornell University Press.

Forrest, P. (2012) On the Argument from Divine Arbitrariness. *Sophia* 51(3). pp. 341–49.

Frankfurt, H. G. (1964) The Logic of Omnipotence. *Philosophical Review* 73(2). pp. 262–63.

Gabriele, L. (2012) Infinitesimals and Infinites in the History of Mathematics: A Brief History. *Applied Mathematics and Computation* 218(16). pp. 7979–88.

Gellman, J. (1998) On a Sociological Challenge to the Veridicality of Religious Experience. *Religious Studies* 34(3). pp. 235–51.

Gregersen, N. H. (2008) Special Divine Action and the Quilt of Laws: Why the Distinction Between Special and General Divine Action Cannot Be Maintained. In Russell, R. J., Murphy, N., & Stoeger, W. R. (eds.) *Scientific Perspectives on Divine Action: Twenty Years of Challenge and Progress*. Vatican City State: Vatican Observatory Publications.

Hacking, I. (1972) The Logic of Pascal's Wager. *American Philosophical Quarterly* 9(2). pp. 186–92.

Harper, L. R. (2013) A Deistic Discussion of Murphy and Tracy's Accounts of God's Limited Activity in the World. *Forum Philosophicum* 18. pp. 93–107.

Harper, L. R. (2014) Evaluating the Fales/Gellman Debate on the Epistemic Status of Mystical Religious Experiences. *International Journal of Philosophy and Theology* 75(1). pp. 55–73.

Harper, L. R. (2015) Epistemic Deism Revisited. *Forum Philosophicum* 20. pp. 51–64.

Harrelson, K. J. (2009) *The Ontological Argument From Descartes to Hegel*. Amherst, NY: Humanity Books.

Hasker, W. (2010) All Too Skeptical Theism. *International Journal for Philosophy of Religion* 68(1). pp. 15–29.

Hefelbower, S. G. (1920) Deism Historically Defined. *The American Journal of Theology* 24(2). pp. 217–23.

Hoffman, J., & Rosenkrantz, G. (2002) *The Divine Attributes*. Oxford: Blackwell.

Holder, R. (2006) Fine Tuning & The Multiverse. *Think* 4(12). pp. 49–60.

Howard-Snyder, D. (1996) *The Evidential Argument From Evil*. Bloomington: Indiana University Press.

Hudson, H. (2005) *The Metaphysics of Hyperspace*. Oxford: Clarendon Press.

Hume, D. (1985) *Of Miracles*. LaSalle: Open Court.

Jacobs, J. (2009) *Naturalism* [Online]. Available from: http://www.iep.utm.edu/naturali/ [Accessed 14 November 2010].

Janzen, G. (2011) Pascal's Wager and the Nature of God. *Sophia* 50. pp. 331–44.

Jefferson, T. (2007) *The Jefferson Bible: The Life and Morals of Jesus of Nazareth.* Radford: A & D Publishing.

Johnson, D. (2013) A Refutation of Skeptical Theism. *Sophia* 52(3). pp. 425–45.

Johnson, D. (2014) The Failure of the Multiverse Hypothesis as a Solution to the Problem of No Best World. *Sophia* 53. pp. 447–65.

Jones, K. (2010) Falsifiability and Traction in Theories of Divine Action. *Zygon* 45(3). pp. 575–89.

Jordan, J. (2006) *Pascal's Wager: Pragmatic Arguments and Belief in God.* Oxford: Clarendon Press.

Kenny, A. (1979) *The God of the Philosophers.* Oxford: Clarendon Press.

Kraay, K. (2010) Theism, Possible Worlds, and the Multiverse. *Philosophical Studies* 147. pp. 355–68.

Kraay, K. (2012) The Theistic Multiverse: Problems and Prospects. In Nagasawa, Y. (ed.) *Scientific Approaches to the Philosophy of Religion.* Houndmills: Palgrave Macmillan.

Krailsheimer, A. J. (1995) *Blaise Pascal: Pensees.* London: Penguin.

Kvanvig, J. L., & McCann, H. J. (1988) Divine Conservation and the Persistence of the World. In Morris, T. (ed.) *Divine & Human Action: Essays in the Metaphysics of Theism.* Ithaca, NY: Cornell University Press.

Larmer, R. (2009) Divine Action and Divine Transcendence. *Zygon* 44(3). pp. 543–57.

Leland, J. (1755) *A View of the Principal Deistical Writers That Have Appeared in England in the Last and Present Century; With Observations Upon Then, and Some Account of the Answers That Have Been Published Against Them. In Several Letters to a Friend.* London: B. Dod.

Lewis, D. (1986) *On the Plurality of Worlds.* Oxford: Blackwell.

Linde, A. D. (1987) Eternally Existing Self-Reproducing Chaotic Inflationary Universe. *Physica Scripta* T15. pp. 169–75.

Linde, A. D. (2000) Inflationary Cosmology. *Physics Reports* 333. pp. 575–91.

Mackie, J. L. (1978) Evil and Omnipotence. In Urban, L. & Walton, D. N. (eds.) *The Power of God: Readings on Omnipotence and Evil.* New York: Oxford University Press.

Mackie, J. L. (1982) *The Miracle of Theism.* Oxford: Clarendon Press.

Manson, N. A. (2003) *God and Design: The Teleological Argument and Modern Science.* London: Routledge.

Mavrodes, G. (1963) Some Puzzles Concerning Omnipotence. *Philosophical Review* 72(2). pp. 221–23.

McHarry, J. D. (1978) A Theodicy. *Analysis* 38. pp. 132–34.

Megill, J. (2011) Evil and the Many Universes Response. *International Journal for Philosophy of Religion* 70. pp. 127–38.

Monton, B. (2012) God Acts in the Quantum World. In Kvanvig, J. L. (ed.) *Oxford Studies in Philosophy of Religion: Volume V.* Oxford: Clarendon Press.

Murphy, N. (1995) Divine Action in the Natural Order: Buridan's Ass and Schrodinger's Cat. In Russell, R. J., Murphy, N., & Peacocke, A. R. (eds.) *Chaos and Complexity: Scientific Perspectives on Divine Action.* Notre Dame, IN: The University of Notre Dame Press.

Nagasawa, Y. (2015) Multiverse Pantheism. In Kraay, K. (ed.) *God and the Multiverse: Scientific, Philosophical, and Theological Perspectives.* New York: Routledge.

Norris, C. (1999) Should Philosophers Take Lessons from Quantum Theory? *Inquiry: An Interdisciplinary Journal of Philosophy* 42. pp. 311–42.

Nowacki, W. R. (2007) *The Kalam Cosmological Argument for God.* Amherst, NY: Prometheus Books.

O'Connor, T. (2008) *Theism and Ultimate Explanation: The Necessary Shape of Contingency.* Melbourne: Wiley-Blackwell.

Oppy, G. (1995) *Ontological Arguments and Belief in God.* New York: Cambridge University Press.

Paley, W. (1848) *Natural Theology, or, Evidences of the Existence and Attributes of the Deity, Collected from the Appearances of Nature.* London: William Milner.

Parfit, D. (1998) The Puzzle of Reality: Why Does the Universe Exist? In van Inwagen, P. & Zimmerman, D. (eds.) *Metaphysics: The Big Questions.* Oxford: Blackwell.

Pike, N. (1970) *God and Timelessness.* New York: Shocken Books.

Plantinga, A. (1965) Free Will Defense. In Black, M. (ed.) *Philosophy in America: Essays.* London: Allen & Unwin.

Pojman, L. (2001) *Philosophy of Religion.* Mountainview, CA: Mayfield.

Ratzsch, D. (2010) Stanford Encyclopedia of Philosophy. *Teleological Arguments for God's Existence* [Online]. Available from: http://plato.stanford.edu/entries/teleological-arguments/ [Accessed 16 September 2013].

Reichenbach, B. (2012) Stanford Encyclopedia of Philosophy. *Cosmological Argument* [Online]. Available from: http://plato.stanford.edu/entried/cosmological-argument/ [Accessed 16 September 2013].

Rescher, N. (1985) *Pascal's Wager: A Study of Practical Reasoning in Philosophical Theology.* Notre Dame, IN: University of Notre Dame Press.

Rowe, W. (1975) *The Cosmological Argument.* Princeton, NJ: Princeton University Press.

Rowe, W. (1979) The Problem of Evil and Some Varieties of Atheism. *American Philosophical Quarterly* 16(4). pp. 335–41.

Rowe, W. (1996) The Evidential Argument from Evil: A Second Look. In Howard-Snyder, D. (ed.) *The Evidential Argument from Evil.* Bloomington: Indiana University Press.

Rowe, W. (2006) Friendly Atheism, Skeptical Theism, and the Problem of Evil. *International Journal for Philosophy of Religion* 59(2). pp. 79–92.

Rowe, W. (2007) *Philosophy of Religion: An Introduction.* Belmont, CA: Wadsworth/Thompson.

Ruse, M. (2003) Biologists and the Argument from Design. In Manson, N. A. (ed.) *God and Design: The Teleological Argument and Modern Science.* London: Routledge.

Saward, M. D. (2013) Fine-Tuning as Evidence for a Multiverse: Why White is Wrong. *International Journal for Philosophy of Religion* 73. pp. 243–53.

Schellenberg, J. L. (2004) Divine Hiddenness Justifies Atheism. In Peterson, M. & van Arragon, R. (eds.) *Contemporary Debates in Philosophy of Religion*. Malden, MA: Blackwell.

Schellenberg, J. L. (2006) *Divine Hiddenness and Human Reason*. Ithaca, NY: Cornell University Press.

Shapiro, S. (2011) Theology and the Actual Infinite: Burley and Cantor. *Theology and Science* 9(1). pp. 101–8.

Sheehy, P. (2006) Theism and Modal Realism. *Religious Studies* 42(3). pp. 315–28.

Smolin, L. (1997) *The Life of the Cosmos*. Oxford: Oxford University Press.

Snapper, J. (2011) Paying the Cost of Skeptical Theism. *International Journal for Philosophy of Religion* 69(1). pp. 45–56.

Sobel, J. H. (1996) Pascalian Wagers. *Synthese* 108. pp. 11–61.

Sober, E. (2003) The Design Argument. In Manson, N. A. (ed.) *God and Design: The Teleological Argument and Modern Science*. London: Routledge.

Steinhardt, P., & Turok, N. (2007) *Endless Universe: Beyond the Big Bang*. New York: Doubleday.

Stewart, M. (1993) *The Greater Good Defense: An Essay on the Rationality of Faith*. New York: St. Martin's Press.

Sullivan, R. (1982) *John Toland and the Deist Controversy: A Study in Adaptations*. Cambridge, MA: Harvard University Press.

Tapp, C. (2011) Infinity in Mathematics and Theology. *Theology and Science* 9(1). pp. 91–100.

Tegmark, M. (2003) Parallel Universes. In Barrow, J. D., Davies, P. C. W., & Harper, C. L. (eds.) *Science and Ultimate Reality: From Quantum to Cosmos, Honoring John Wheeler's 90th Birthday*. Cambridge: Cambridge University Press.

Tegmark, M. (2007) The Multiverse Hierarchy. In Carr, B. (ed.) *Universe or Multiverse?* Cambridge: Cambridge University Press.

Tracy, T. F. (1995) Particular Providence and the God of the Gaps. In Russel, R. J., Murphy, N., & Peacocke, A. R. (eds.) *Chaos and Complexity: Scientific Perspectives on Divine Action*. Notre Dame, IN: The University of Notre Dame Press.

Trakakis, N. (1997) The Absolutist Theory of Omnipotence. *Sophia* 36. pp. 55–78.

Turner, D. (2004) The Many-Universes Solution to the Problem of Evil. In Gale, M. & Pruss, A. (eds.) *The Existence of God*. Aldershot: Ashgate.

Vaidman, L. (2008) *Many-Worlds Interpretation of Quantum Mechanics* [Online]. Available from: http://plato.stanford.edu/archives/fall2008/entries/qm-manyworlds/ [Accessed 7 October 2010].

Vailati, E. (1998) *Samuel Clarke: A Demonstration of the Being and Attributes of God*. Cambridge: Cambridge University Press.

Van Inwagen, P. (1982) The Incompatibility of Free Will and Determinism. In Watson, G. (ed.) *Free Will*. Oxford: Oxford University Press.

Veneziano, G. (2006) The Myth of the Beginning of Time. *Scientific American* 16(1). pp. 71–81.

Wainwright, W. (1987) *Philosophy of Religion*. Belmont, CA: Wadsworth.

Wallace, D. (2012) *The Emergent Multiverse: Quantum Theory According to the Everett Interpretation.* Oxford: Oxford University Press.
Webb, C. (1929) *Pascal's Philosophy of Religion.* Oxford: Clarendon Press.
White, R. (2003) Fine-Tuning and Multiple Universes. In Manson, N. A. (ed.) *God and Design: The Teleological Argument and Modern Science.* London: Routledge.
Wierenga, E. (1989) *The Nature of God: An Inquiry Into Divine Attributes.* Ithaca, NY: Cornell University Press.
Wilkinson, T. (2013) Fine Tuning the Multiverse. *Think* 12(33). pp. 89–101.

Index

Adams, Robert, 30, 112
Ahern, M. B., 80
arbitrariness, 36–37, 52, 62–65, 101

Bristow, William, 50, 121

Cameron, Ross, 117
the cosmological argument, 72, 74–76
Craig, William Lane, 74–75

Descartes, René, 52
the design argument, 27, 29, 72, 110–11
determinism, 38, 40–43, 93
Deutsch, David, 17–18
divine attributes: eternality, 60–61; immutability, 51, 61; necessity, 51, 60–61, 108, 115; omnibenevolence, 12, 26–27, 33–34, 41, 51, 56–59, 61–62, 64, 77, 79, 80–81, 117; omnipotence, 26, 51–54, 56, 62–63, 79–81, 100–101, 126–27; omniscience, 26, 36, 39–40, 51, 53–54, 59–60, 62–63, 79–81, 101; timelessness, 51, 60–61
divine intervention, 34–37, 41, 48, 55–56, 62–65, 77, 82–84, 90–92, 94, 96–103, 113–14, 119–20
deism: epistemic, 78, 89–91, 93, 97, 99, 102–4; metaphysical, 91, 97–99, 104

efficiency, 54–56, 62–63, 126

the fine-tuning argument, 10–11, 21
free will, 12–13, 38, 39–43, 81

God of the gaps, 94
Gregersen, Niels, 113–14
GRW theory, 95–96, 101–2

Hefelbower, S. G., 48
hiddenness, the argument from divine, 76–79, 117, 126
Hoffman, Joshua, 60
Hudson, Hud, 10–11
Hume, David, 83, 85
hyperspace, 10–11

Jefferson, Thomas, 120
Jones, Kile, 113

Kraay, Klaas, 11–12
Kvanvig, Jonathan, 48

Larmer, Robert, 91–92, 97
laws of nature, 16–18, 21, 40–43, 48, 50, 54–55, 64, 81–85, 90–93, 95, 97–98, 101
Lewis, David, 30, 112–13
Linde, A. D., 18–19
location of God, 20, 49, 99, 115–17

Mackie, J. L., 80
Manson, Neil, 72
Mavrodes, George, 52–54
McCann, Hugh, 48
Megill, Jason, 9–10
miracles, 50, 82–86, 91–93, 96–98, 120–22, 126
modal realism, 30, 32, 112, 115
Monton, Bradley, 91–93, 95–96, 101–2, 104
morality, 27–30, 78, 109, 112–13, 120–21
motivation, 37, 53–54, 63–65, 96
Murphy, Nancey, 91–102, 104

Nagasawa, Yujin, 30, 112
noninterventionist special divine action, 89–92, 95, 102, 104–5
Norris, Christopher, 17–18

the ontological argument, 73–74
Oppy, Graham, 73

paradox of the stone, 52–53
personal relationship with God, 76–77, 117–19, 128
petitionary prayer, 128
Pike, Nelson, 60
praiseworthiness, 113, 127–28
principle of sufficient reason, 75, 93, 97

the problem of evil, 9–10, 21, 41, 59, 79, 80–82, 126
propositional knowledge, 59
psuedo-tasks, 53–54, 56, 62

Ratzsch, Dal, 71–72
Rosenkrantz, Gary, 60
Rowe, William, 80
Ruse, Michael, 41

Schellenberg, J. L., 77–78
self-reproducing universes, 18–19
Sheehy, Paul, 115, 117
skeptical theism, 58–59
Sober, Elliot, 72

Tegmark, Max, 15–18
the teleological argument, 71–73
theistic multiverse, 11–12, 30
Tracy, Thomas, 91–92, 94–96, 99–102, 104
Trakakis, Nick, 52
Turner, Donald, 10

van Inwagen, Peter, 40

wavepacket, 18, 27
White, Roger, 110
Wierenga, Edward, 60
Wilkinson, Tim, 15, 20

About the Author

Dr. Leland Royce Harper is assistant professor of philosophy at Siena Heights University. Having been awarded his PhD from the University of Birmingham, Dr. Harper has presented his work at numerous international philosophy conferences and has published essays in the philosophy of religion, the philosophy of race, aesthetics, and epistemology.